Ninja Foodi Air Fryer Cookbook for Beginners 2021

Easy & Delicious Air Fry, Dehydrate, Roast, Bake, Reheat, and More Recipes for Beginners and Advanced Users

Helen Bently

TABLE OF CONTENTS

Chapter 6-Seafood and Fish Recipes 55

Chapter 7-Vegetables Recipes 68

Chapter 8-Desserts Recipes 78

Chapter 9-3 Weeks Diet Plan 88

Conclusion 92

Chapter 1- Ninja Foodi Air Fryer

The Ninja Foodi Air fryer is yet another extraordinary and remarkable kitchen appliance that pulls out crispy yet delicious meals in no time, especially for those with an on-to-go lifestyle.

The ninja Foodi air fryer surely helps prepare low-fat meals that in return positively affect our health. The ninja air fryer is an essential appliance to prepare healthy meals without compromising taste, texture, and health.

The ninja Foodi air fryer cooks food by circulating hot air around the food; as a result, crispy and crunchy food is prepared with less than a teaspoon of oil. So, now you can enjoy guilt-free food that uses 75 percent less fat than a traditional frying method.

The temperature range for the appliance is 105 degrees to 400 degrees F, which makes it possible to remove the outer moisture from the food and make it crispy outside and juicy inside.

If you're on a budget and find it hard to spend the extra dollar to buy a separate appliance to dehydrate, roast, air fry, or even dehydrate, then worry no more, this budget-oriented appliance does multiple functions with a hand free and odor free cooking experience.

In this cookbook we are covering the following:

- Introduction
- The Functions of Air Fryer
- How to Use the Air Fryer
- Maintaining and Cleaning the Appliance
- Many delicious and mouth-watering recipes
- 3-week diet plan
- Conclusion

Along with the 100+ recipes, we have added beautiful images of the recipes and snippets of the nutritional information, so that the overall calorie intake process stays on right track. The recipes that are part of this cookbook that helps all the beginners prepare scrumptious meals using a variety of ninja air fryer functions.

Now, lets the journey begin.

What is Ninja Foodi Air Fryer?

Meet one of the highly demanded and top-rated appliances that can air fry, air roast, reheat, and dehydrate your favorite food items in a much easy and fast way.

Now you can easily cook 2 pounds of French fries with just a teaspoon of oil. The ninja Foodi Air fryer provides a convenient way to prepare a family meal with its reasonably large basket. The ninja air fryer incorporates a smart button that allows the user to choose any function with just one touch.

The Ninja Foodi Air fryer is easily available at an affordable price on Amazon, online, and local stores.

The Functions of Ninja Air Fryer

This Ninja Air fryer includes a ceramic crisper plate and a ceramic-coated basket. It has an Air Outlet Unit, main unit, a control panel, and air intake vent.

Ninja® Air Fryer Function

Air Fry: You can use this function to prepare crunchy and crispy food with little or no oil.
Air Roast: The roast unit prepares some tender meat and baked treats.
Reheat: Revive your leftover by warming it to crispy perfection.
Dehydrate: Now you can easily dehydrate the fruits and vegetables to prepare some easy snacks.

Operating Buttons

TEMP arrows you can up and down the temp arrows to adjust the cooking temperature.
TIME arrows: The time arrows are used to adjust the cooking time in any function.
START/PAUSE button: Once the time and temperature are selected for the specific recipe the START/PAUSE button starts cooking, pressing it again during the cooking stops the cooking process.
POWER button: The Power button shuts off the unit.
STANDBY MODE: After 10 minutes if no interaction is done with the control panel, the unit gets into a standby mode.

How to Use Ninja Air Fryer

The use of Ninja Foodi air fryer is easy as a touch of a button.
First, it is very crucial to grease the basket with oil spray.
You need to follow the recipe properly and do not overcrowd the basket.
You simply add the food to the basket and select the required function like AIR FRY, AIR roast, dehydrate or reheat.

Then adjust the cooking time and temperature using the operational buttons.
Once the food gets cooked, you can take out the basket and transfer the food to serving plates.

Maintaining and Cleaning the Appliance

- When using for the first time, discard all the packaging and wash the basket and other accessories that come with an air fryer.
- It is very important to read the instructional manual.
- It is highly recommended to pay attention to all the warnings, operational instructions, tips, and safeguards to avoid appliance damage or personal injury.
- It is not recommended to clean the main unit in the dishwasher.
- The accessories of the appliance are dishwasher safe and can be washed using the dishwasher.
- The Ninja air fryer is only intended to be used indoor.
- Remember to check the voltage indications are corresponding to the main voltage from the switch.
- It is not recommended to immerse the appliance in water.
- Keep the cord away from the reach of children and hot areas like stoves, heaters, etc.
- When operating, it's not recommended to touch the outer surface of the air fryer.
- Place the air fryer on a horizontal, sturdy, and flat surface.
- Unplug the appliance once done.
- Using any other accessory attachments that are not recommended by SharkNinja may cause electric shock, fire, or even injury.
- It is not recommended to use an air fryer for deep-frying with the oil.
- Make sure that the basket is closed before operating.
- Do not use a damaged cord or plugs to operate the appliance.
- Spilled food after cooking can cause serious burns, so wash the basket and clean the appliance after every use.

Cleaning of Air Fryer

- Let the appliance cool down properly before cleaning, then unplug the power cord of the air fryer.
- Make sure the appliance is properly cool down before cleaning.
- You can clean the outer surface by using a damp towel.
- Clean the inside of the air fryer with a nonabrasive sponge.
- The basket, crisper plate, and any other accessories can be easily washed in the dishwasher.
- Any food residue stuck to the basket can be cleaned by placing in the sink and filling it with soapy warm water for 5 minutes, then remove the residual with a soft sponge.

Chapter 2-Breakfast Recipes

Sweet Potatoes Hash

Prep: 15 Minutes | Cook Time: 25 Minutes | Makes: 2 Servings

Ingredients

- 450 grams sweet potatoes
- 1/2 white onion, diced
- 3 tablespoons of olive oil
- 1 teaspoon smoked paprika
- 1/4 teaspoon cumin
- 1/3 teaspoon of ground turmeric
- 1/4 teaspoon of garlic salt
- 1 cup guacamole

Directions

1. Preheat the unit by selecting AIR FRY mode for 3 minutes at 325 degrees F.
2. Select START/PAUSE to begin the preheating process.
3. Once preheating is done, press START/PAUSE.
4. Peel and cut the potatoes into cubes.
5. Now, transfer the potatoes to a bowl and add oil, white onions, cumin, paprika, turmeric, and garlic salt.
6. Put this mixture into the basket of the Ninja Foodi Air Fryer.
7. Set it to AIR FRY mode for 10 minutes at 390 degrees F.
8. Then take out the basket and shake them well.
9. Then again set time to 15 minutes at 390 degrees F.
10. Once done, serve it with guacamole.
11. Serving Suggestion: serve it with ketchup and omelet
12. Variation Tip: Use canola oil instead of olive oil

Nutritional Information Per Serving: Calories691 | Fat 49.7g| Sodium 596mg | Carbs 64g | Fiber15g | Sugar 19g | Protein 8.1g

Egg and Avocado in The Ninja Foodi

Prep: 10 Minutes | Cook Time: 10 Minutes | Makes: 2 Servings

Ingredients

- 2 Avocados, pitted and cut in half
- Garlic salt, to taste
- Cooking for greasing
- 4 eggs
- ¼ teaspoon of Paprika powder, for sprinkling
- 1/3 cup parmesan cheese, crumbled
- 6 bacon strips, raw

Directions

1. Preheat the unit by selecting AIR FRY mode for 3 minutes at 325 degrees F.
2. Select START/PAUSE to begin the preheating process.
3. Once preheating is done, press START/PAUSE.
4. Next, cut the avocado in half and pit it.
5. Now scoop out the flesh from the avocado and keep intact some of it.
6. Crack one egg in each hole of avocado and sprinkle paprika and garlic salt
7. Top it with cheese at the end.
8. Now pour it into tin foil and then put it in the air fryer basket along with bacon strips.
9. Set it to AIR FRY mode at 400 degrees F for 10 minutes..
10. Once done, serve and enjoy.

Serving Suggestion: Serve it with Bread slices

Variation Tip: Use butter for greasing

Nutritional Information Per Serving: Calories609 | Fat53.2g | Sodium 335mg | Carbs 18.1g | Fiber13.5g | Sugar 1.7g | Protein 21.3g

Bacon and Egg Omelet

Prep: 12 Minutes | Cook Time: 10 Minutes | Makes: 2 Servings

Ingredients

- 2 eggs, whisked
- ½ teaspoon of chopped tomatoes
- Sea Salt and black pepper, to taste
- 2 teaspoons of almond milk
- 1 teaspoon of cilantro, chopped
- 1 small green chili, chopped
- 4 slices of bacon

Directions

1. Take a bowl and whisk eggs in it.
2. Then add green chili, salt, black pepper, cilantro, almond milk, and chopped tomatoes.
3. Oil greases two ramekins.
4. Pour this into ramekins.
5. Preheat the unit by selecting AIR FRY mode for 4 minutes at 325 degrees F.
6. Select START/PAUSE to begin the preheating process.
7. Once preheating is done, put the ramekins inside the unit along with bacon slices.
8. Set it to AIR FRY mode at 400 degrees F, for 10 minutes
9. Once 7minutes pass, take out the basket and remove the bacon from the unit.
10. Again press start, to finish the cooking time.
11. Once done take out the eggs from the ramekins and serve with bacons strip.
12. Enjoy hot.

Serving Suggestion: Serve it with bread slices and ketchup

Variation Tip: Use garlic salt instead of sea salt

Nutritional Information Per Serving: Calories 285| Fat 21.5g| Sodium1000 mg | Carbs 2.2g | Fiber 0.1g| Sugar1 g | Protein 19.7g

Breakfast Sausage Omelet

Prep: 10 Minutes | Cook Time: 15 Minutes | Makes: 2 Servings

Ingredients

- ¼ pound breakfast sausage, cooked and crumbled
- 4 eggs, beaten
- ½ cup pepper Jack cheese blend
- 2 tablespoons green bell pepper, sliced
- 1 green onion, chopped
- 1 pinch cayenne pepper
- Cooking spray

Directions

1. Take a bowl and whisk eggs in it along with crumbled sausage, pepper Jack cheese, green onions, red bell pepper, and cayenne pepper.
2. Mix it all well.
3. Take cake pan that fit inside the Ninja air fryer and grease it with oil spray.
4. Pour the omelet mixture into the cake pan.
5. Preheat the unit by selecting AIR FRY mode for 3 minutes at 325 degrees F.
6. Select START/PAUSE to begin the preheating process.
7. Once preheating is done, put the cake pan inside the basket and place the basket inside the unit.
8. Turn on the BAKE function and let it cook for 15-20 minutes at 310 degrees F.
9. Once the cooking cycle completes, take out, and serve hot, as a delicious breakfast.

Serving Suggestion: Serve it with ketchup

Variation Tip: Use Parmesan cheese instead of pepper jack Cheese

Nutritional Information Per Serving: Calories 691| Fat52.4g | Sodium1122 mg | Carbs 13.3g | Fiber 1.8g| Sugar 7g | Protein 42g

Banana and Raisins Muffins

Prep: 20 Minutes | Cook Time: 16 Minutes | Makes: 2 Servings

Ingredients

- Salt, pinch
- 2 eggs, whisked
- 1/3 cup butter, melted
- 4 tablespoons of almond milk
- ¼ teaspoon of vanilla extract
- ½ teaspoon of baking powder
- 1-1/2 cup all-purpose flour
- 1 cup mashed bananas
- 2 tablespoons of raisins

Directions

1. Preheat the unit by selecting AIR FRY mode for 3 minutes at 325 degrees F.
2. Select START/PAUSE to begin the preheating process.
3. Once preheating is done, press START/PAUSE.
4. Take about 4 large (one-cup sized) ramekins and layer them with muffin papers.
5. Crack eggs in a large bowl, and whisk it all well and start adding vanilla extract, almond milk, baking powder, and melted butter
6. Whisk the ingredients very well.
7. Take a separate bowl and add the all-purpose flour, and salt.
8. Now, combine the add dry ingredients with the wet ingredients.
9. Now, pour mashed bananas and raisins into this batter
10. Mix it well to make a batter for the muffins.
11. Now pour the batter into 4 ramekins and place the ramekins in the air fryer basket.
12. Set the timer to 16 minutes at 350 degrees F at AIRFRY mode.
13. Check if not done, and let it AIR FRY for one more minute.
14. Once it is done, serve.

Serving Suggestion: None

Variation Tip: None

Nutritional Information Per Serving: Calories 727| Fat 43.1g| Sodium366 mg | Carbs 74.4g | Fiber 4.7g | Sugar 16.1g | Protein 14.1g

Bacon and Eggs for Breakfast

Prep: 12 Minutes | Cook Time: 12 Minutes | Makes: 1 Serving

Ingredients

- 4 strips of thick-sliced bacon
- 2 small eggs
- Salt and black pepper, to taste
- Oil spray for greasing ramekins

Directions

1. Take 2 ramekins and grease them with oil spray.
2. Crack eggs in a bowl and season it salt and black pepper.
3. Divide the egg mixture between two ramekins.
4. Preheat the unit by selecting AIR FRY mode for 3 minutes at 325 degrees F.
5. Select START/PAUSE to begin the preheating process.
6. Once preheating is done, put the ramekin inside the bottom of the air fryer basket, and bacon on side.
7. Put the basket inside the unit.
8. Now set it to AIR FRY mode at 400 degrees F, for 12 minutes.
9. Press start to begin the cooking.
10. Once done, serve and enjoy.

Serving Suggestion: None

Variation Tip: Use butter for greasing ramekins

Nutritional Information Per Serving: Calories131 | Fat 10g| Sodium 187mg | Carbs0.6 g | Fiber 0g | Sugar 0.6g | Protein 10.7

Breakfast Casserole

Prep: 5 Minutes | Cook Time: 10 Minutes | Makes: 4 Servings

Ingredients

- 1 pound of beef sausage, grounded
- 1/4 cup diced white onion
- 1 diced green bell pepper
- 8 whole eggs, beaten
- ½ cup Colby jack cheese, shredded
- ¼ teaspoon of garlic salt
- Oil spray, for greasing

Directions

1. Take a bowl and add ground sausage to it.
2. Add in the diced onions, bell peppers, eggs and whisk it well.
3. Then season it with garlic salt.
4. Spray the basket of the air fryer with oil spray.
5. Preheat the unit by selecting AIR FRY mode for 5 minutes at 325 degrees F.
6. Select START/PAUSE to begin the preheating process.
7. Once preheating is done, place the mixture inside the basket; remember to remove the crisper plate.
8. Top the mixture with cheese.
9. Now, turn ON the Ninja Foodi Air Fryer and select AIR FRY mode and set the time to 10 minutes at 390 degrees F.
10. Once the cooking cycle completes, take out, and serve.
11. Serve and enjoy.

Serving Suggestion: Serve it with sour cream

Variation Tip: Use turkey sausages instead of beef sausages.

Nutritional Information Per Serving: Calories 699| Fat 59.1g | Sodium 1217 mg | Carbs 6.8g | Fiber 0.6g| Sugar 2.5g | Protein33.1 g

Sausage with Eggs

Prep: 10 Minutes | Cook Time: 12 Minutes | Makes: 2 Servings

Ingredients

- 4 sausage links, raw and uncooked
- 4 eggs, uncooked
- 1 tablespoon of green onion
- 2 tablespoons of chopped tomatoes
- Salt and black pepper, to taste
- 2 tablespoons of milk, dairy
- Oil spray, for greasing

Directions

1. Take a bowl and whisk eggs in it.
2. Then pour milk, and add onions and tomatoes.
3. Whisk it all well.
4. Now season it with salt and black pepper.
5. Take one cake pan, that fit inside the air fryer and grease it with oil spray.
6. Pour the omelet in the greased cake pans.
7. Slice the sausages in round shapes and top it on eggs.
8. Preheat the unit by selecting AIR FRY mode for 3 minutes at 325 degrees F.
9. Select START/PAUSE to begin the preheating process.
10. Once preheating is done, put the cake pan inside the unit.
11. Select bake function of ninja air fryer, and set the timer to 12 minutes at 310 degrees F.
12. Once the cooking cycle completes, serve by transferring it to plates.
13. Enjoy hot as a delicious breakfast.

Serving Suggestion: Serve it with toasted bread slices

Variation Tip: Use almond milk if like non-dairy milk

Nutritional Information Per Serving: Calories 240 | Fat 18.4g| Sodium 396mg | Carbs 2.8g | Fiber0.2g | Sugar 2g | Protein 15.6g

Egg with Baby Spinach

Prep: 12 Minutes | Cook Time: 12 Minutes | Makes: 4 Servings

Ingredients

- Nonstick spray, for greasing ramekins
- 2 tablespoons olive oil
- 6 ounces baby spinach
- 2 garlic cloves, minced
- 1/3 teaspoon kosher salt
- 6-8 large eggs
- ½ cup half and half
- Salt and black pepper, to taste
- 8 Sourdough bread slices, toasted

Directions

1. Preheat the unit by selecting AIR FRY mode for 2 minutes at 350 degrees F.
2. Select START/PAUSE to begin the preheating process.
3. Once preheating is done, press START/PAUSE.
4. Grease 4 ramekins with oil spray and set aside for further use.
5. Take a skillet and heat oil in it.
6. Then cook spinach for 2 minutes and add garlic and salt black pepper.
7. Let it simmer for2more minutes.
8. Once the spinach is wilted, transfer it to a plate.
9. Whisk an egg into a small bowl.
10. Add in the spinach.
11. Whisk it well and then pour half and half.
12. Divide this mixture between 4 ramekins and remember not to overfill it to the top, leave a little space on top.
13. Put the ramekins in the basket of the Ninja Foodi Air Fryer.
14. Press start and select AIR fry mode at 350 degrees F for 12 minutes.
15. Once it's cooked and eggs are done, serve with sourdough bread slices.

Serving Suggestion: Serve it with cream cheese topping

Variation Tip: Use plain bread slices instead of sourdough bread slices.

Nutritional Information Per Serving: Calories 404| Fat 19.6g| Sodium 761mg | Carbs 40.1g | Fiber 2.5g| Sugar 2.5g | Protein 19.2g

Yellow Potatoes with Eggs

Prep: 10 Minutes | Cook Time: 30 Minutes | Makes: 2 Servings

Ingredients

- 1 pound of Dutch yellow potatoes, quartered
- 1 red bell pepper, chopped
- Salt and black pepper, to taste
- 1 green bell pepper, chopped
- 2 teaspoons of olive oil
- 2 teaspoons of garlic powder
- 1 teaspoon of onion powder
- 1 egg
- ¼ teaspoon of butter

Directions

1. Preheat the unit by selecting AIR FRY mode for 5 minutes at 325 degrees F.
2. Select START/PAUSE to begin the preheating process.
3. Once preheating is done, press START/PAUSE.
4. Toss together diced potatoes, green pepper, red pepper, salt, black pepper, and olive oil along with garlic powder and onion powder.
5. Take ramekin and grease it with oil spray.
6. Whisk egg in a bowl and add salt and pepper along with ½ teaspoon of butter.
7. Pour egg into a ramekin and place ramekins inside the air fryer.
8. Transfer bowl ingredients to the air fryer basket aside the ramekins.
9. Set the timer for basket to 30 minutes at 400 degrees F, on the AIR FRY mode.
10. Once10 minutes pass press START/PAUSE and takeout the ramekin.
11. Press the start button, and let the potato cook for remaining minutes.
12. Once done, serve and enjoy.

Serving Suggestion: Serve it with sourdough toasted bread slices

Variation Tip: Use white potatoes instead of yellow Dutch potatoes.

Nutritional Information Per Serving: Calories252 | Fat7.5g | Sodium 37mg | Carbs 40g | Fiber3.9g | Sugar 7g | Protein 6.7g

Chapter 3-Snacks and Appetizers Recipes

Strawberries and Walnuts Muffins

Prep: 15 Minutes | Cook Time: 15 Minutes | Makes: 2 Servings

Ingredients

- Salt, pinch
- 2 eggs, whisked
- 1/3 cup maple syrup
- 1/3 cup coconut oil
- 4 tablespoons of water
- 1 teaspoon of orange zest
- ¼ teaspoon of vanilla extract
- ½ teaspoon of baking powder
- 1 cup all-purpose flour
- 1 cup strawberries, finely chopped
- 1/3 cup walnuts, chopped and roasted

Directions

1. Preheat the unit by selecting AIR FRY mode for 2 minutes at 325 degrees F.
2. Select START/PAUSE to begin the preheating process.
3. Once preheating is done, press START/PAUSE.
4. Take one cup size of 4 ramekins that are oven safe.
5. Layer it with muffin paper.
6. In a bowl and add egg, maple syrup, oil, water, vanilla extract, and orange zest.
7. Whisk it all very well
8. In a separate bowl, mix flour, baking powder, and salt.
9. Now add dry ingredients slowly to wet ingredients.
10. Now pour this batter into ramekins and top it with strawberries and walnuts.
11. Now put ramekins inside basket of air fryer and set the time to 15 minutes at 350 degrees F.
12. Check if not done let it AIR FRY for one more minute.
13. Once done, serve.

Serving Suggestion: serve it with coffee

Variation Tip: use vegetable oil instead of coconut oil

Nutritional Information Per Serving: Calories 897| Fat 53.9g | Sodium 148mg | Carbs 92g | Fiber 4.7g| Sugar35.6 g | Protein 17.5g

Stuffed Bell Peppers

Prep: 25 Minutes | Cook Time: 16 Minutes | Makes: 3 Servings

Ingredients

- 6 large bell peppers
- 1-1/2 cup cooked rice
- 2 cups cheddar cheese

Directions

1. Preheat the unit by selecting AIR FRY mode for 5 minutes at 350 degrees F.
2. Select START/PAUSE to begin the preheating process.
3. Once preheating is done, press START/PAUSE.
4. Cut the bell peppers in half lengthwise and remove all the seeds.
5. Fill the cavity of each bell pepper with cooked rice.
6. Grease the basket of air fryer with oil spray
7. Transfer the bell peppers to the basket of the Ninja air fryer.
8. Set the time for 200 degrees for 10 minutes.
9. Afterward, take out the basket and sprinkle cheese on top.
10. Set the time at 200 degrees for 6 minutes.
11. Once it's done, serve.

Serving Suggestion: Serve it with mashed potato

Variation Tip: You can use any cheese you like

Nutritional Information Per Serving: Calories 605| Fat 26g | Sodium477 mg | Carbs68.3 g | Fiber4 g| Sugar 12.5g | Protein25.6 g

Spicy Chicken Tenders

Prep: 15 Minutes | Cook Time: 12 Minutes | Makes: 2 Servings

Ingredients

- 2 large eggs, whisked
- 2 tablespoons lemon juice
- Salt and black pepper
- 1 pound of chicken tenders
- 1 cup Panko breadcrumbs
- 1/2 cup Italian bread crumb
- 1 teaspoon smoked paprika
- 1/4 teaspoon garlic powder
- 1/4 teaspoon onion powder
- 1/2 cup fresh grated parmesan cheese

Directions

1. Preheat the unit by selecting AIR FRY mode for 2 minutes at 325 degrees F.
2. Select START/PAUSE to begin the preheating process.
3. Once preheating is done, press START/PAUSE.
4. Take a bowl and whisk eggs in it and set aside for further use.
5. In a large bowl add lemon juice, paprika, salt, black pepper, garlic powder, onion powder
6. In a separate bowl mix Panko breadcrumbs, Italian bread crumbs, and parmesan cheese.
7. Dip the chicken tenders in the spice mixture and coat the entire tender well.
8. Let the tenders sit for 1 hour.
9. Then dip each chicken tender in egg and then in bread crumbs.
10. Line the basket of the air fryer with parchment paper.
11. Transfer the tenders to the basket.
12. Set it to air fry mode at 350 degrees F for 12 minutes.
13. Once it's done, serve.

Serving Suggestion: Serve it with ketchup

Variation Tip: Use mild paprika instead of smoked paprika

Nutritional Information Per Serving: Calories 836| Fat 36g| Sodium1307 mg | Carbs 31.3g | Fiber 2.5g| Sugar3.3 g | Protein 95.3g

Sweet Bites

Prep: 25 Minutes | Cook Time: 10 Minutes | Makes: 4 Servings

Ingredients

- 10 sheets of Phyllo dough, (filo dough)
- 2 tablespoons of melted butter
- 1 cup walnuts, chopped
- 2 teaspoons of honey
- Pinch of cinnamon
- 1 teaspoon of orange zest

Directions

1. Preheat the unit by selecting AIR FRY mode for 2 minutes at 325 degrees F.
2. Select START/PAUSE to begin the preheating process.
3. Once preheating is done, press START/PAUSE.
4. First, layer together 10 Phyllo dough sheets on a flat surface.
5. Then cut it into 4 *4-inch squares.
6. Now, coat the squares with butter, drizzle some honey, orange zest, walnuts, and cinnamon.
7. Bring all 4 corners together and press the corners to make a little like purse design.
8. Put it inside the air fryer basket and select the AIR fry mode and set it for 10 minutes at 375 degrees F.
9. Once done, take out and serve.

Serving Suggestion: Serve with a topping of nuts

Variation Tip: None

Nutritional Information Per Serving: Calories 397| Fat 27.1 g| Sodium 271mg | Carbs31.2 g | Fiber 3.2g| Sugar3.3g | Protein 11g

Parmesan Crush Chicken

Prep: 20 Minutes | Cook Time: 18 Minutes | Makes: 4 Servings

Ingredients

- 4 chicken breasts
- 1 cup parmesan cheese
- 1 cup bread crumb
- 2 eggs, whisked
- Salt, to taste
- Oil spray, for greasing

Directions

1. Preheat the unit by selecting AIR FRY mode for 5 minutes at 325 degrees F.
2. Select START/PAUSE to begin the preheating process.
3. Once preheating is done, press START/PAUSE.
4. Whisk egg in a large bowl and set aside.
5. Season the chicken breast with salt and then put it in egg wash.
6. Next, dredge it in breadcrumb then parmesan cheese.
7. Line the basket of the air fryer with parchment paper.
8. Put the breast pieces inside the basket, and oil spray the breast pieces.
9. Set it to air fry mode at 350 degrees F, for 18 minutes.
10. Once it's done, serve.

Serving Suggestion: Serve it with ketchup

Variation Tip: Use cheddar cheese instead of parmesan

Nutritional Information Per Serving: Calories574 | Fat25g | Sodium848 mg | Carbs 21.4g | Fiber 1.2g| Sugar 1.8g | Protein 64.4g

Dijon Cheese Sandwich

Prep: 10 Minutes | Cook Time: 10 Minutes | Makes: 2 Servings

Ingredients

- 4 large slices sourdough, whole grain
- 4 tablespoons of Dijon mustard
- 1-1/2 cup grated sharp cheddar cheese
- 2 teaspoons green onion, chopped the green part
- 2 tablespoons of butter melted

Directions

1. Preheat the unit by selecting AIR FRY mode for 2 minutes at 325 degrees F.
2. Select START/PAUSE to begin the preheating process.
3. Once preheating is done, press START/PAUSE.
4. Brush the melted butter on one side of all the bread slices.
5. Then spread Dijon mustard on other sides of slices.
6. Then top the 2 bread slices with cheddar cheese and top it with green onions.
7. Cover with the remaining two slices to make two sandwiches.
8. Put it to the basket of the air fryer.
9. Turn on the air fry mode at 350 degrees f, for 10 minutes.
10. Once it's done, serve.

Serving Suggestion: Serve with tomato soup

Variation Tip: Use oil spray instead of butter

Nutritional Information Per Serving: calories 617| fat 38 g| sodium 1213mg | carbs40.8 g | fiber 5g| sugar 5.6g | protein 29.5g

Cheddar Quiche

Prep: 10 Minutes | Cook Time: 12 Minutes | Makes: 2 Servings

Ingredients

- 4 eggs, organic
- 1-1/4 cup heavy cream
- Salt, pinch
- ½ cup broccoli florets
- ½ cup cheddar cheese, shredded and for sprinkling

Directions

1. Take a Pyrex pitcher and crack two eggs in it.
2. And fill it with heavy cream, about half the way up.
3. Add in the salt and then add in the broccoli and pour this into a quiche dish, and top it with shredded cheddar cheese.
4. Preheat the unit by selecting AIR FRY mode for 2 minutes at 325 degrees F.
5. Select START/PAUSE to begin the preheating process.
6. Once preheating is done, press START/PAUSE.
7. Now put the dish inside air fryer basket.
8. Set the time to 12 minutes at 325 degrees F.
9. Once done, serve hot.

Serving Suggestion: Serve with herbs as a topping

Variation Tip: Use spinach instead of broccoli florets

Nutritional Information Per Serving: Calories 454| Fat40g | Sodium 406mg | Carbs 4.2g | Fiber 0.6g| Sugar1.3 g | Protein 20g

Grill Cheese Sandwich

Prep: 15 Minutes | Cook Time: 10 Minutes | Makes: 2 Servings

Ingredients

- 4 slices of white bread slices
- 2 tablespoons of butter, melted
- 2 slices of sharp cheddar
- 2 slices of Swiss cheese
- 2 slices of mozzarella cheese

Directions

1. Preheat the unit by selecting AIR FRY mode for 2 minutes at 325 degrees F.
2. Select START/PAUSE to begin the preheating process.
3. Once preheating is done, press START/PAUSE.
4. Brush melted butter on one side of all the bread slices and then top the 2 bread slices with slices of cheddar, Swiss, and mozzarella, one slice per bread.
5. Top it with the other slice to make a sandwich.
6. Add it to the basket of the air fryer.
7. Turn on AIR FRY mode at 350 degrees F for 10 minutes.
8. Once done, serve.

Serving Suggestion: Serve with tomato soup

Variation Tip: Use oil spray instead of butter

Nutritional Information Per Serving: Calories 577 | Fat38g | Sodium 1466mg | Carbs 30.5g | Fiber 1.1g| Sugar 6.5g | Protein 27.6g

Blueberries Muffins

Prep: 15 Minutes | Cook Time: 15 Minutes | Makes: 2 Servings

Ingredients

- Salt, pinch
- 2 eggs
- 1/3 cup sugar
- 1/3 cup vegetable oil
- 4 tablespoons of water
- 1 teaspoon of lemon zest
- ¼ teaspoon of vanilla extract
- ½ teaspoon of baking powder
- 1 cup all-purpose flour
- 1 cup blueberries

Directions

1. Take 4 one-cup sized ramekins that are oven safe and layer them with muffin papers.
2. Take a bowl and whisk the egg, sugar, oil, water, vanilla extract, and lemon zest.
3. Whisk it all very well.
4. Now, in a separate bowl, mix the flour, baking powder, and salt.
5. Now, add dry ingredients slowly to wet ingredients.
6. Now, pour this batter into ramekins and top it with blueberries.
7. Preheat the unit by selecting AIR FRY mode for 2 minutes at 325 degrees F.
8. Select START/PAUSE to begin the preheating process.
9. Once preheating is done, press START/PAUSE.
10. Now, place the ramekins inside the Ninja Foodi Air Fryer.
11. Set the time to AIRFRY mode for 15 minutes at 350 degrees F.
12. Check if not done, and let it AIR FRY for one more minute.
13. Once it is done, serve.

Serving Suggestion: Serve it with whipped cream topping

Variation Tip: use butter instead of vegetable oil

Nutritional Information Per Serving: Calories 781| Fat41.6g | Sodium 143mg | Carbs 92.7g | Fiber 3.5g| Sugar41.2 g | Protein 0g

Chicken Tenders

Prep: 15 Minutes | Cook Time: 12 Minutes | Makes: 3 Servings

Ingredients

- 1 pound of chicken tender
- Salt and black pepper, to taste
- 1 cup Panko bread crumbs
- 2 cups Italian bread crumbs
- 1 cup parmesan cheese
- 2 eggs
- Oil spray, for greasing

Directions

1. Sprinkle the tenders with salt and black pepper.
2. In a medium bowl mix Panko bread crumbs with Italian breadcrumbs.
3. Add salt, pepper, and parmesan cheese.
4. Crack two eggs in a bowl.
5. First, put the chicken tender in eggs.
6. Now dredge the tender in a bowl and coat the tender well with crumbs.
7. Preheat the unit by selecting AIR FRY mode for 2 minutes at 325 degrees F.
8. Select START/PAUSE to begin the preheating process.
9. Once preheating is done, press START/PAUSE.
10. Line the basket of the air fryer with parchment paper.
11. At the end spray the tenders with oil spray.
12. Layer the tenders inside the basket of Ninja Foodi Air Fryer.
13. Set it to the AIR FRY mode at 350 degrees F for 12 minutes.
14. Once it's done, serve.

Serving Suggestion: Serve it with ranch or ketchup

Variation Tip: Use Italian seasoning instead of Italian bread crumbs

Nutritional Information Per Serving: Calories558 | Fat23.8g | Sodium872 mg | Carbs 20.9g | Fiber1.7 g| Sugar2.2 g | Protein 63.5g

Chapter 4-Beef, Lamb and Pork Recipes

Ham Burger Patties

Prep: 15 Minutes | Cook Time: 16 Minutes | Makes: 2 Serving

Ingredients

- 1 pound of ground beef
- Salt and pepper, to taste
- ½ teaspoon of red chili powder
- ¼ teaspoon of coriander powder
- 2 tablespoons of chopped onion
- 1 green chili, chopped
- Oil spray for greasing
- 2 large potato wedges

Directions

1. Take out the rack and oil greases the air fryer basket with oil spray.
2. Add potato wedges in the basket.
3. Put the rack on top and cover it with aluminum foil.
4. Take a bowl and add minced beef in it and add salt, pepper, chili powder, coriander powder, green chili, and chopped onion.
5. Mix well and make two burger patties with wet hands.
6. Put the patties beside wedges inside air fryer.
7. Now, set time for 12 minutes using AIR FRY mode at 400 degrees F.
8. Once the time of cooking complete, take out the basket.
9. Flip the patties and turn and twist the potatoes wedges.
10. Again, set time for 4 minutes at 400 degrees F
11. Once it's done, serve and enjoy.

Serving Suggestion: Serve it with bread slices, cheese, and pickles, lettuce, and onion

Variation Tip: None

Nutritional Information Per Serving: Calories875 | Fat21.5g | Sodium 622mg | Carbs 88g | Fiber10.9 g| Sugar 3.4g | Protein 78.8g

Bell Peppers with Sausages

Prep: 15 Minutes | Cook Time: 15 Minutes | Makes: 4 Servings

Ingredients

*   6 beef or pork Italian sausages
*   4 bell peppers, whole
*   Oil spray, for greasing
*   2 cups of cooked rice
*   1 cup of sour cream

Directions

1. Preheat the unit by selecting AIR FRY mode for 2 minutes at 325 degrees F.
2. Select START/PAUSE to begin the preheating process.
3. Once preheating is done, press START/PAUSE.
4. Put the bell pepper inside the basket and sausages accommodating aside.
5.   Now, place the basket inside the unit.
6. Set it to AIR FRY MODE for 15 minutes at 400 degrees F.
7. Once done and serve over cooked rice with a dollop of sour cream.

Serving Suggestion: Serve it with salad

Variation Tip: use olive oil instead of oil spray.

Nutritional Information Per Serving: Calories1356 | Fat 81.2g| Sodium 3044 mg | Carbs 96g | Fiber 3.1g | Sugar 8.3g | Protein 57.2 g

Pork Chops

Prep: 10 Minutes | Cook Time: 20 Minutes | Makes: 2 Servings

Ingredients

- 1 tablespoon of rosemary, chopped
- Salt and black pepper, to taste
- 2 garlic cloves
- 1-inch ginger
- 2 tablespoons of olive oil
- 8 pork chops

Directions

1. Take a blender and pulse together rosemary, salt, pepper, garlic cloves, ginger, and olive oil.
2. Rub this marinade over pork chops and let it rest for 1 hour.
3. Then adjust it inside the air fryer and set it to AIR FRY mode for 20 minutes at 375 degrees F.
4. Once the cooking cycle is done, take out and serve hot.

Serving Suggestion: Serve it with salad

Variation Tip: Use canola oil instead of olive oil

Nutritional Information Per Serving: Calories 1154| Fat 93.8g| Sodium 225mg | Carbs 2.1g | Fiber0.8 g| Sugar 0g | Protein 72.2g

Spicy Lamb Chops

Prep: 15 Minutes | Cook Time: 15 Minutes | Makes: 4 Servings

Ingredients

- 12 lamb chops, bone-in
- Salt and black pepper, to taste
- ½ teaspoon of lemon zest
- 1 tablespoon of lemon juice
- 1 teaspoon of paprika
- 1 teaspoon of garlic powder
- ½ teaspoon of Italian seasoning
- ¼ teaspoon of onion powder

Directions

1. Preheat the unit by selecting AIR FRY mode for 2 minutes at 325 degrees F.
2. Select START/PAUSE to begin the preheating process.
3. Once preheating is done, press START/PAUSE.
4. Add the lamb chops to the bowl and sprinkle salt, garlic powder, Italian seasoning, onion powder, black pepper, lemon zest, lemon juice, and paprika.
5. Rub the chops well, and transfer it to the basket of the air fryer.
6. Set the air fryer at 400 degrees F, for 15 minutes at AIR FRY mode.
7. After 10 minutes, take out the basket and flip the chops.
8. Cook for the remaining minutes, and then serve.

Serving Suggestion: Serve it over rice

Variation Tip: None

Nutritional Information Per Serving: Calories 787| Fat 45.3g| Sodium1 mg | Carbs 16.1g | Fiber0.3g | Sugar 0.4g | Protein 75.3g

Short Ribs & Root Vegetables

Prep: 15 Minutes | Cook Time: 45 Minutes | Makes: 2 Servings

Ingredients

- 1 pound of beef short ribs, bone-in and trimmed
- Salt and black pepper, to taste
- 2 tablespoons canola oil, divided
- 1/4 cup red wine
- 3 tablespoons brown sugar
- 2 cloves garlic, peeled, minced
- 4 carrots, peeled, cut into 1-inch pieces
- 2 parsnips, peeled, cut into 1-inch pieces
- ½ cup pearl onions

Directions

1. Preheat the unit by selecting AIR FRY mode for 5 minutes at 325 degrees F.
2. Select START/PAUSE to begin the preheating process.
3. Once preheating is done, press START/PAUSE.
4. Season the ribs with salt and black pepper and rub a little amount of canola oil on both sides.
5. Place it in the basket of the air fryer.
6. Next, take a bowl and add pearl onions, parsnip, carrots, garlic, brown sugar, red wine, salt, and black pepper.
7. Add the vegetable mixture over the ribs.
8. Set the basket time to 45 minutes at 390 degrees F at AIR FRY mode.
9. Hit start so the cooking cycle being.
10. Once the cooking complete, take out the ingredient and serve short ribs with the mixed vegetables and liquid collect at the bottom of basket.
11. Enjoy it hot.

Serving Suggestion: Serve it with mashed potatoes

Variation Tip: Use olive oil instead of canola oil.

Nutritional Information Per Serving: Calories1262 | Fat 98.6g| Sodium 595mg | Carbs 57g | Fiber 10.1g| Sugar 28.2g | Protein 35.8g

Chinese BBQ Pork

Prep: 15 Minutes | Cook Time: 25-35 Minutes | Makes: 2 Servings

Sauce Ingredients

- 4 tablespoons of soy sauce
- ¼ cup red wine
- 2 tablespoons of oyster sauce
- ¼ tablespoons of hoisin sauce
- ¼ cup honey
- ¼ cup brown sugar
- Pinch of salt
- Pinch of black pepper
- 1 teaspoon of ginger garlic, paste
- 1 teaspoon of five-spice powder

Other Ingredients

- 1.5 pounds of pork shoulder, sliced

Directions

1. Take a bowl and mix all the ingredients listed under sauce ingredients.
2. Transfer half of it to a sauce pan and let it cook for 10 minutes.
3. Set it aside.
4. Let the pork marinate in the remaining sauce for 2 hours.
5. Afterward, put the pork slices in the basket and set it to AIRFRY mode 450 degrees for 25 minutes.
6. Make sure the internal temperature is above 160 degrees F once cooked.
7. If not add a few more minutes to the overall cooking time.
8. Once done, take it out and baste it with prepared sauce.
9. Serve and Enjoy.

Serving Suggestion: Serve it with rice

Variation Tip: Skip the wine and add vinegar

Nutritional Information Per Serving: Calories 1239| Fat 73 g| Sodium 2185 mg | Carbs 57.3 g | Fiber 0.4g| Sugar53.7 g | Protein 81.5 g

Glazed Steak Recipe

Prep: 15 Minutes | Cook Time: 25 Minutes | Makes: 2 Servings

Ingredients

- 1 pound of beef steaks
- ½ cup, soy sauce
- Salt and black pepper, to taste
- 1 tablespoon of vegetable oil
- 1 teaspoon of grated ginger
- 4 cloves garlic, minced
- 1/4 cup brown sugar

Directions

1. Take a bowl and whisk together soy sauce, salt, pepper, vegetable oil, garlic, brown sugar, and ginger.
2. Once a paste is made rub the steak with the marinate
3. Let it sit for 30 minutes.
4. After 30 minutes add the steak to the air fryer basket and set it to AIR FRY mode at 400 degrees F for 18-22 minutes.
5. After 10 minutes, hit pause and takeout the basket.
6. Let the steak flip and again let it AIR FRY for the remaining minutes.
7. Once 25 minutes of cooking cycle completes.
8. Take out the steak and let it rest. Serve by cutting into slices.
9. Enjoy.

Serving Suggestion: Serve it with mashed potatoes

Variation Tip: Use canola oil instead of vegetable oil

Nutritional Information Per Serving: Calories 563| Fat 21 g| Sodium 156mg | Carbs 20.6g | Fiber0.3 g| Sugar17.8 g | Protein69.4 g

Steak and Mashed Creamy Potatoes

Prep: 15 Minutes | Cook Time: 45-50 Minutes | Makes: 1 Serving

Ingredients

- 2 Russet potatoes, peeled and cubed
- ¼ cup butter, divided
- 1/3 cup heavy cream
- ½ cup shredded cheddar cheese
- Salt and black pepper, to taste
- 1 New York strip steak, about a pound
- 1 teaspoon of olive oil
- Oil spray, for greasing

Directions

1. Preheat the unit by selecting AIR FRY mode for 5 minutes at 350 degrees F.
2. Select START/PAUSE to begin the preheating process.
3. Once preheating is done, press START/PAUSE.
4. Rub the potatoes with salt and a little amount of olive oil about a teaspoon.
5. Next, season the steak with salt and black pepper.
6. Place the russet potatoes along with steak in basket of air fryer.
7. Oil sprays the steak and set it to AIR fry mode for 50 minutes, at 375 degrees F.
8. Hit start and Lethe ninja Foodi do its magic.
9. One 12 minutes pass, take out the steak and let the cooking cycle completes.
10. Afterward take out potato and mash the potatoes and then add butter, heavy cream, and cheese along with salt and black pepper.
11. Serve the mashed potatoes with steak.
12. Enjoy.

Serving Suggestion: Serve it with rice

Variation Tip: Use Parmesan instead of cheddar

Nutritional Information Per Serving: Calories1932 | Fat 85.2g| Sodium 3069mg | Carbs 82g | Fiber10.3 g| Sugar 5.3g | Protein 22.5g

Steak in Air Fry

Prep: 15 Minutes | Cook Time: 22 Minutes | Makes: 1 Serving

Ingredients

- 2 teaspoons of canola oil
- 1 tablespoon of Montreal steaks seasoning
- 1 pound of beef steak

Directions

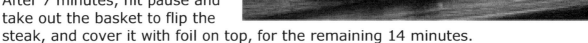

1. The first step is to season the steak on both sides with canola oil and then rub a generous amount of steak seasoning all over.

2. Put the steak in the basket and set it to AIR FRY mode at 450 degrees F for 22 minutes.

3. After 7 minutes, hit pause and take out the basket to flip the steak, and cover it with foil on top, for the remaining 14 minutes.

4. Once done, serve the medium-rare steak and enjoy it by resting for 10 minutes.

5. Serve by cutting in slices.

6. Enjoy.

Serving Suggestion: Serve it with mashed potatoes

Variation Tip: Use vegetable oil instead of canola oil.

Nutritional Information Per Serving: Calories 935| Fat 37.2g| Sodium 1419mg | Carbs 0g | Fiber 0g| Sugar 0g | Protein137.5 g

Beef & Broccoli

Prep: 12 Minutes | Cook Time: 12 Minutes | Makes: 4 Servings

Ingredients

- 12 ounces of teriyaki sauce, divided
- ½ tablespoon garlic powder
- ¼ cup of soy sauce
- 1 pound raw sirloin steak, thinly sliced
- 2 cups broccoli, cut into florets
- 2 teaspoons of olive oil
- Salt and black pepper, to taste

Directions

1. Preheat the unit by selecting AIR FRY mode for 7 minutes at 350 degrees F.
2. Select START/PAUSE to begin the preheating process.
3. Once preheating is done, press START/PAUSE.
4. Take a zip-lock plastic bag and mix teriyaki sauce, salt, garlic powder, black pepper, soy sauce, and olive oil.
5. Marinate the beef in it for 2 hours.
6. Then drain the beef from the marinade.
7. Now toss the broccoli with oil, teriyaki sauce, and salt and black pepper.
8. Put the ingredients inside the air fryer basket.
9. Set it to AIRFRY mode at 390 degrees F, for 12 minutes.
10. Hit start and let the cooking cycle completes.
11. Once it's done take out the beef and broccoli and serve immediately with leftover teriyaki sauce and cooked rice.

Serving Suggestion: Serve it with mashed potatoes

Variation Tip: Use canola oil instead of olive oil

Nutritional Information Per Serving: Calories 344| Fat 10g| Sodium 4285mg | Carbs18.2 g | Fiber 1.5g| Sugar 13.3g | Protein42 g

Yogurt Lamb Chops

Prep: 10 Minutes | Cook Time: 22 Minutes | Makes: 2 Servings

Ingredients

- 1½ cups plain Greek yogurt
- 1 lemon, juice only
- 1 teaspoon ground cumin
- 1 teaspoon ground coriander
- ¾ teaspoon ground turmeric
- ¼ teaspoon ground allspice
- 10 rib lamb chops (1–1¼ inches thick cut)
- 2 tablespoons olive oil, divided

Directions

1. Take a bowl and add lamb chop along with listed ingredients.
2. Rub the lamb chops well.
3. and let it marinate in the refrigerator for 1 hour.
4. Afterward takeout the lamb chops from the refrigerator.
5. Layer parchment paper inside basket
6. Put the chops inside basket and place the basket inside the unit.
7. Set the time to 22 minutes at 400 degrees F.
8. Hit start and then wait for the chop to be cooked.
9. Once the cooking is done, take out the lamb chops and let the chops serve on plates.

Serving Suggestion: Serve over rice

Variation Tip: Use canola oil instead of olive oil

Nutritional Information Per Serving: Calories1973 | Fat90 g| Sodium228 mg | Carbs 109.2g | Fiber 1g | Sugar 77.5g | Protein 184g

Beef Ribs I

Prep: 10 Minutes | Cook Time: 18 Minutes | Makes: 2 Servings

Ingredients

- 4 tablespoons of barbecue spice rub
- 1 tablespoon kosher salt and black pepper
- 3 tablespoons brown sugar
- 2 pounds of beef ribs (3-3 1/2 pounds), cut in thirds
- 1 cup barbecue sauce

Directions

1. In a small bowl, add salt, pepper, brown sugar, and BBQ spice rub.
2. Grease the ribs with oil spray from both sides and then rub it with a spice mixture.
3. Adjust the ribs inside the Ninja Air fryer, and set it to AIR FRY MODE at 375 degrees F for 18 minutes.
4. Hit start and let the air fryer cook the ribs.
5. Once done, serve with the coating BBQ sauce.

Serving Suggestion: Serve it with salad and baked potato

Variation Tip: Use sea salt instead of kosher salt

Nutritional Information Per Serving: Calories1081 | Fat 28.6 g| Sodium 1701mg | Carbs 58g | Fiber 0.8g| Sugar 45.7g | Protein 138 g

Beef Ribs II

Prep: 20 Minutes | Cook Time: 1 Hour | Makes: 2 Servings

Ingredients for Marinade

- ¼ cup olive oil
- 4 garlic cloves, minced
- ½ cup white wine vinegar
- ¼ cup soy sauce, reduced-sodium
- ¼ cup Worcestershire sauce
- 1 lemon juice
- Salt and black pepper, to taste
- 2 tablespoons of Italian seasoning
- 1 teaspoon of smoked paprika
- 2 tablespoons of mustard
- ½ cup maple syrup

Meat Ingredients

- Oil spray, for greasing
- 8 beef ribs lean

Directions

1. Preheat the unit by selecting AIR FRY mode for 2 minutes at 325 degrees F.
2. Select START/PAUSE to begin the preheating process.
3. Once preheating is done, press START/PAUSE.
1. Take a large bowl and add all the ingredients under marinade ingredients.
2. Put the marinade in a zip lock bag and add ribs to it.
3. Let it sit for 4 hours.
4. Now take out the basket of air fryer and grease the basket with oil spray.
5. Now put the ribs in the basket.
6. Set it to AIR fry mode at 220 degrees F for 30 minutes.
7. Select Pause and take out the basket.
8. Afterward, flip the ribs and cook for 30 more minutes at 250 degrees F.
9. Once done, serve the juicy and tender ribs.
10. Enjoy.

Serving Suggestion: Serve it with Mac and cheese

Variation Tip: Use garlic-infused oil instead of garlic cloves

Nutritional Information Per Serving: Calories 1927| Fat116g| Sodium 1394mg | Carbs 35.2g | Fiber 1.3g| Sugar29 g | Protein 172.3g

Chapter 5-Chicken and Poultry Recipes

Glazed Thighs with French Fries

Prep: 22 Minutes | Cook Time: 35 Minutes | Makes: 3 Servings

Ingredients

- 2 tablespoons of Soy Sauce
- Salt, to taste
- 1 teaspoon of Worcestershire Sauce
- 2 teaspoons Brown Sugar
- 1 teaspoon of Ginger, paste
- 1 teaspoon of Garlic, paste
- 6 Boneless Chicken Thighs
- 1 pound of hand-cut potato fries (thick)
- 2 tablespoons of canola oil

Directions

1. Coat the French fries well with canola oil.
2. Season it with salt.
3. In a small bowl, combine the soy sauce, Worcestershire sauce, brown sugar, ginger, and garlic.
4. Place the chicken in this marinade and let it sit for 40 minutes.
5. Put the chicken thighs and potatoes into the basket.
6. Set it to AIR FRY mode at 390 degrees F for 25-35 minutes.
7. Once the cooking cycle completely take out the fries and chicken and serve it hot.

Serving Suggestion: Serve it with ketchup

Variation Tip: You can use honey instead of brown sugar

Nutritional Information Per Serving: Calories 858| Fat39g | Sodium 1509mg | Carbs 45.6g | Fiber 4.4g | Sugar3 g | Protein 90g

Sweet and Spicy Carrots with Chicken Thighs

Prep: 15 Minutes | Cook Time: 25 Minutes | Makes: 2 Servings

Ingredients

Ingredients for Glaze

- Cooking spray, for greasing
- 2 tablespoons butter, melted
- 1 tablespoon hot honey
- 1 teaspoon orange zest
- 1 teaspoon cardamom
- ½ pound baby carrots
- 1 tablespoon orange juice
- Salt and black pepper, to taste

Other Ingredients

- ½ pound of carrots, baby carrots
- 8 chicken thighs

Directions

1. Take a bowl and mix all the glaze ingredients in it.
2. Now, coat the chicken and carrots with the glaze and let it rest for 30 minutes.
3. Now place the chicken thighs and carrots into the air fryer basket.
4. Press start and set it to ROAST Mode at 390 degrees F for 25 minutes.
5. After 12 minutes, take out the carrots and let the cooking cycle completes for chicken.
6. Then serve it hot.

Serving Suggestion: Serve with Salad

Variation Tip: Use lime juice instead of orange juice.

Nutritional Information Per Serving: Calories 1312| Fat 55.4g| Sodium 757mg | Carbs 23.3g | Fiber6.7 g | Sugar12 g | Protein171 g

Wings with Corn on Cob

Prep: 15 Minutes | Cook Time: 25 Minutes | Makes: 2 Servings

Ingredients

- 6 chicken wings, skinless
- 2 tablespoons of coconut amino
- 2 tablespoons of brown sugar
- 1 teaspoon of ginger, paste
- ½ inch garlic, minced
- Salt and black pepper to taste
- 2 corn on cobs, small
- Oil spray, for greasing

Directions

1. Spay the corns with oil spray and season them with salt.
2. Rub the ingredients well.
3. Coat the chicken wings with coconut amino, brown sugar, ginger, garlic, salt, and black pepper.
4. Spray the wings with a good amount of oil spray.
5. Now put the chicken wings in the basket, along with corns.
6. Select AIRFRY function and set time to 25 minutes at 390 degrees F.
7. After 15 minutes take out the corn
8. Let the cooking cycle complete for the chicken.
9. Once it's done, serve and enjoy.

Serving Suggestion: Serve it with garlic butter sauce

Variation Tip: use butter instead of oil spray.

Nutritional Information Per Serving: Calories 950| Fat33.4g | Sodium592 mg | Carbs27. 4g | Fiber2.1g | Sugar11.3 g | Protein129 g

Yummy Chicken Breasts

Prep: 15 Minutes | Cook Time: 25 Minutes | Makes: 2 Servings

Ingredients

- 4 large chicken breasts, 6 ounces each
- 2 tablespoons of oil bay seasoning
- 1 tablespoon Montreal chicken seasoning
- 1 teaspoon of thyme
- 1/2 teaspoon of paprika
- Salt, to taste
- oil spray, for greasing

Directions

1. Season the chicken breast pieces with the listed seasoning and let them rest for 40 minutes.
2. Grease both sides of the chicken breast pieces with oil spray.
3. Put the chicken breast pieces inside the basket.
4. Set the AIRFRY mode at 400 degrees F, for 15 minutes.
5. Select pause and take out the basket and flip the chicken breast pieces, after 15 minutes.
6. Select air fry at 400 degrees F, for 10 more minutes.
7. Once it's done serve.

Serving Suggestion: Serve it with baked potato

Variation Tip: None

Nutritional Information Per Serving: Calories 711| Fat 27.7g| Sodium 895mg | Carbs 1.6g | Fiber 0.4g | Sugar 0.1g | Protein 106.3g

Chicken Thighs with Brussels sprouts

Prep: 20 Minutes | Cook Time: 30 Minutes | Makes: 2 Servings

Ingredients

- 2 tablespoons of honey
- 4 tablespoons of Dijon mustard
- Salt and black pepper, to tat
- 4 tablespoons of olive oil
- 1-1/2 cup Brussels sprouts
- 8 chicken thighs, skinless

Directions

1. Take a bowl and add chicken thighs to it.
2. Add honey, Dijon mustard, salt, pepper, and 2 tablespoons of olive oil to the thighs.
3. Coat the chicken well and marinate it for 1 hour.
4. Now when start cooking season the Brussels sprouts with salt and black pepper along with remaining olive oil.
5. Put the chicken along with the Brussels sprouts into the basket.
6. Select ROAST function and set time to 30 minutes at 390 degrees F.
7. Once done, serve and enjoy.

Serving Suggestion: Serve it with Barbecue Sauce

Variation Tip: You can use canola oil instead of olive oil.

Nutritional Information Per Serving: Calories1454 | Fat 72.2g| Sodium 869mg | Carbs 23g | Fiber 2.7g | Sugar 19g | Protein 172g

Chicken & Broccoli

Prep: 22 Minutes | Cook Time: 22 Minutes | Makes: 2 Servings

Ingredients

- 1 pound of chicken, boneless & bite-size pieces
- 1-1/2 cup of broccoli
- 2 tablespoons of Grape seed oil
- 1/3 teaspoon of garlic powder
- 1 teaspoon of ginger and garlic paste
- 2 teaspoons of soy sauce
- 1 tablespoon of sesame seed oil
- 2 teaspoons rice vinegar
- Salt and black pepper, to taste
- Oil spray, for coating

Directions

1. Take a small bowl and whisk together Grape seed oil, ginger and garlic paste, sesame seeds oil, rice vinegar, and soy sauce.
2. Take a large bowl and mix chicken pieces with the prepared marinade.
3. Let it sit for 1 hour.
4. Now, slightly grease the broccoli with oil spray and season it with salt and black pepper.
5. Put the broccoli and chicken into the basket of the air fryer that is greased with oil spray.
6. Set it to AIR FRY mode at 390 degrees F, for 22 minutes.
7. After 8 minutes of cooking, press the START/PAUSE button and takes out the broccoli.
8. Keep continuing with the chicken cooking process.
9. Once the cooking time completes, take out the chicken and serve it with the broccoli.

Serving Suggestion: Serve it with lemon wedges

Variation Tip: A light oil alternative can be used as grape seed oil.

Nutritional Information Per Serving: Calories588 | Fat 32.1g| Sodium 457mg | Carbs 4g | Fiber1.3 g | Sugar 1g | Protein67.4 g

Chicken Leg Piece

Prep: 15 Minutes | Cook Time: 25 Minutes | Makes: 1 Serving

Ingredients

- 1 teaspoon of onion powder
- 1 teaspoon of paprika powder
- 1 teaspoon of garlic powder
- Salt and black pepper, to taste
- 1 tablespoon of Italian seasoning
- 1 teaspoon of celery seeds
- 2 eggs, whisked
- 1/3 cup buttermilk
- 1 cup of corn flour
- 1 pound of chicken leg

Directions

1. Take a bowl and whisk egg along with pepper, salt, and buttermilk.
2. Set it aside for further use.
3. Mix all the spices in a small separate bowl.
4. Dredge the chicken in egg wash then dredge it in seasoning.
5. Coat the chicken legs with oil spray.
6. At the end dust it with the corn flour.
7. Put the leg pieces into air fryer basket.
8. Set it to 400 degrees F, for 25 minutes.
9. Let the air fryer do the magic.
10. Once it's done, serve and enjoy.

Serving Suggestion: Serve it with cooked rice

Variation Tip: Use water instead of buttermilk.

Nutritional Information Per Serving: Calories 1511| Fat 52.3g| Sodium615 mg | Carbs 100g | Fiber 9.2g | Sugar 8.1g | Protein 154.2g

Spiced Chicken and Vegetables

Prep: 22 Minutes | Cook Time: 35 Minutes | Makes: 1 Serving

Ingredients

- 2 large chicken breasts
- 2 teaspoons of olive oil
- 1 teaspoon of chili powder
- 1 teaspoon of paprika powder
- 1 teaspoon of onion powder
- ½ teaspoon of garlic powder
- 1/4 teaspoon of Cumin
- Salt and black pepper, to taste

Vegetable Ingredients

- 2 large potato, cubed
- 4 large carrots cut into bite-size pieces
- 1 tablespoon of olive oil
- Salt and black pepper, to taste

Directions

1. Take chicken breast pieces and rub olive oil, salt, pepper, chili powder, onion powder, cumin, garlic powder, and paprika.
2. Season the vegetables with olive oil, salt, and black pepper.
3. Now put the chicken breast pieces along with vegetables inside the air fryer basket.
4. Now set it to AIR FRY mode at 390 degrees F, for 35 minutes.
5. Once the cooking cycle is done, serve, and enjoy.

Serving Suggestion: Serve it with salad or ranch dressing

Variation Tip: Use Canola oil instead of olive oil.

Nutritional Information Per Serving: Calories1510 | Fat 51.3g| Sodium 525mg | Carbs 163g | Fiber24.7 g | Sugar 21.4g | Protein 102.9

Cornish Hen with Baked Potatoes

Prep: 20 Minutes | Cook Time: 45 Minutes | Makes: 2 Servings

Ingredients

- Salt, to taste
- 1 large potato
- 1 tablespoon of avocado oil
- 1.5 pounds of Cornish hen, skinless and whole
- 2-3 teaspoons of poultry seasoning, dry rub

Directions

1. Take a fork and pierce the large potato.
2. Rub the potato with avocado oil and salt.
3. Now put the potatoes in the bottom of basket.
4. Now pick the Cornish hen and season the hen with poultry seasoning (dry rub) and salt.
5. Remember to coat the whole Cornish hen well.
6. Now place the hen over the potatoes inside the basket.
7. Now set it to AIR FRY mode at 350 degrees F, for 45 minutes.
8. Once the cooking cycle complete, turn off the air fryer and take out the potatoes and Cornish hen from the air fryer basket.
9. Serve hot and enjoy.

Serving Suggestion: Serve it with Coleslaw

Variation Tip: You can use olive oil or canola oil instead of avocado oil.

Nutritional Information Per Serving: Calories 612 | Fat14.3 g| Sodium 304mg | Carbs33.4 g | Fiber 4.5 g | Sugar 1.5g | Protein 83.2 g

Chicken Breast Strips

Prep: 10 Minutes | Cook Time: 22 Minutes | Makes: 2 Servings

Ingredient

- 2 large organic egg
- 1-ounce buttermilk
- 1 cup of cornmeal
- ¼ cup all-purpose flour
- Salt and black pepper, to taste
- 1 pound of chicken breasts, cut into strips
- 2 tablespoons of oil bay seasoning
- oil spray, for greasing

Directions

1. Take a medium bowl and whisk eggs with buttermilk.
2. In a separate large bowl mix flour, cornmeal, salt, black pepper, and oil bay seasoning.
3. First, dip the chicken breast strip in egg wash and then dredge into the flour mixture.
4. Coat the strip all over and layer it inside the basket that is already grease with oil spray.
5. Grease the chicken breast strips with oil spray as well.
6. Set the basket to AIR FRY mode at 400 degrees F for 22 minutes.
7. Hit the start button to let the cooking start.
8. Once the cooking cycle is done, serve.

Serving Suggestion: Serve it with roasted vegetables

Variation Tip: None

Nutritional Information Per Serving: Calories 788| Fat25g| Sodium835 mg | Carbs60g | Fiber 4.9g| Sugar1.5g | Protein79g

Cornish Hen with Asparagus

Prep: 20 Minutes | Cook Time: 45 Minutes | Makes: 2 Servings

Ingredients

- 10 spears of asparagus
- Salt and black pepper, to taste
- 1 Cornish hen
- Salt, to taste
- Black pepper, to taste
- 1 teaspoon of Paprika
- Coconut spray, for greasing
- 2 lemons, sliced

Directions

1. Wash and pat dry the asparagus and coat it with coconut oil spray.
2. Sprinkle salt on the asparagus and place inside the bottom of the basket of the air fryer.
3. Next, take the Cornish hen and rub it well with the salt, black pepper, and paprika.
4. Oil sprays the Cornish hen and place it on top of asparagus inside the air fryer basket.
5. Set the time to 45 minutes at 350 degrees F, by selecting the ROAST mode.
6. Once the 6 minutes pass hit START/PAUSE button and take out the asparagus.
7. put the basket back in unit.
8. Once the chicken cooking cycle complete, transfer chicken to the serving plate
9. Serve the chicken with roasted asparagus and slices of lemon.
10. Serve hot and enjoy.

Serving Suggestion: Serve it with ranch dressing

Variation Tip: You can add variation by choosing chopped cilantro instead of a lemon slice.

Nutritional Information Per Serving: Calories 192| Fat 4.7g| Sodium 151mg | Carbs10.7 g | Fiber 4.6g | Sugar 3.8g | Protein 30g

Spicy Chicken

Prep: 12 Minutes | Cook Time: 35-40 Minutes | Makes: 4 Servings

Ingredients

- 4 chicken thighs
- 2 cups of butter milk
- 4 chicken legs
- 2 cups of flour
- Salt and black pepper, to taste
- 2 tablespoons garlic powder
- ½ teaspoon onion powder
- 1 teaspoon poultry seasoning
- 1 teaspoon cumin
- 2 tablespoons paprika
- 1 tablespoon olive oil

Directions

1. Take a bowl and add buttermilk to it.
2. Soak the chicken thighs and chicken legs in the buttermilk for 2 hours.
3. Mix flour, all the seasonings, and olive oil in a small bowl.
4. Take out the chicken pieces from the buttermilk mixture and then dredge them into the flour mixture.
5. Repeat the steps for all the pieces and then arrange it into the air fryer basket.
6. Set the timer by selecting a roast mode for 35-40 minutes at 350 degrees F.
7. Once the cooking cycle complete select the pause button and then take out the basket.
8. Serve and enjoy.

Serving Suggestion: Serve the chicken with garlic dipping sauce

Variation Tip: Use canola oil instead of olive oil

Nutritional Information Per Serving: Calories 624| Fat17.6 g| Sodium300 mg | Carbs 60g | Fiber 3.5g | Sugar 7.7g | Protein54.2 g

Spice-Rubbed Chicken Pieces

Prep: 22 Minutes | Cook Time: 40 Minutes | Makes: 6 Servings

Ingredients

- 3 pounds chicken, pieces
- 1 teaspoon sweet paprika
- 1 teaspoon mustard powder
- 1 tablespoon brown sugar, dark
- Salt and black pepper, to taste
- 1 teaspoon Chile powder, New Mexico
- 1 teaspoon oregano, dried
- ¼ teaspoon allspice powder, ground

Directions

1. Take a bowl and mix dark brown sugar, salt, paprika, mustard powder, oregano, Chile powder, black pepper, and all spice powder.
2. Mix well and rub this spice mixture all over the chicken.
3. Put the chicken into the air fryer basket.
4. Oil sprays the chicken from top.
5. Now set the time to 40 minutes at 350 degrees F.
6. Now press start and once the cooking cycle completes, press stop.
7. Take out the chicken and serve hot.

Serving Suggestion: Serve it with coleslaw, peanut sauce, or ranch

Variation Tip: use light brown sugar instead of dark brown sugar.

Nutritional Information Per Serving: Calories353 | Fat 7.1g| Sodium400 mg | Carbs 2.2g | Fiber0.4 g | Sugar 1.6g | Protein66 g

Chicken Wings

Prep: 15 Minutes | Cook Time: 20 Minutes | Makes: 3 Servings

Ingredients

- 1 cup chicken batter mix, Louisiana
- 9 Chicken wings
- ½ teaspoon of smoked paprika
- 2 tablespoons of Dijon mustard
- 1 tablespoon of cayenne pepper
- 1 teaspoon of meat tenderizer, powder
- oil spray, for greasing

Directions

1. Pat dry chicken wings, and add mustard, paprika, meat tenderizer, and cayenne pepper.
2. Dredge it in the chicken batter mix.
3. Oil sprays the chicken wings.
4. Grease the basket of the air fryer.
5. Put the wings into the air fryer.
6. Set it to AR FRY mode at 400 degrees F for 20 minutes
7. Hit start to begin with the cooking.
8. Once the cooking cycle complete, serve, and enjoy hot.

Serving Suggestion: Serve it with salad

Variation Tip: use American yellow mustard instead of Dijon mustard

Nutritional Information Per Serving: Calories621 | Fat 32.6g| Sodium 2016mg | Carbs 46.6g | Fiber 1.1g | Sugar 0.2g | Protein 32.1g

Chapter 6-Seafood and Fish Recipes

Seafood Shrimp Omelet

Prep: 20 Minutes | Cook Time: 15 Minutes | Makes: 2 Servings

Ingredient

- 6 large shrimp, shells removed and chopped
- 6 eggs, beaten
- ½ tablespoon of butter, melted
- 2 tablespoons green onions, sliced
- 1/3 cup of mushrooms, chopped
- 1 pinch paprika
- Salt and black pepper, to taste
- Oil spray, for greasing

Directions

1. In a large bowl whisk the eggs and add chopped shrimp, butter, green onions, mushrooms, paprika, salt, and black pepper.
2. Take a cake pan that fit inside the air fryer and grease them with oil spray.
3. Pour the egg mixture in the cake pan and place it inside the basket of the air fryer.
4. Turn on the BAKE function, and let it cook for 15 minutes at 320 degrees F.
5. Once the cooking cycle completes, take out, and serve hot.

Serving Suggestion: Serve it with rice

Variation Tip: use olive oil for greasing purposes

Nutritional Information Per Serving: Calories 300 | Fat 17.5g| Sodium 368mg | Carbs 2.9g | Fiber 0.3g | Sugar1.4 g | Protein32.2 g

Salmon with Broccoli and Cheese

Prep: 15 Minutes | Cook Time: 15 Minutes | Makes: 2 Servings

Ingredients

- 2 cups of broccoli
- ½ cup of butter, melted
- Salt and pepper, to taste
- Oil spray, for greasing
- 1 cup of grated cheddar cheese
- 1 pound of salmon, fillets

Directions

1. Take a bowl and add broccoli to it.
2. Add salt and black pepper and spray it with oil.
3. Put the broccoli in the basket.
4. Now rub the salmon fillets with salt, black pepper, and butter.
5. Put fish and broccoli inside the basket.
6. Then insert the basket into the unit.
7. Set it to air fry mode for 15 minters at 400 degrees F.
8. Hit start to start the cooking.
9. Once done, serve by placing it on serving plates.
10. Put the grated cheese on top of the salmon, enjoy.

Serving Suggestion: Serve it with rice and baked potato

Variation Tip: Use olive oil instead of butter

Nutritional Information Per Serving: Calories 966 | Fat 79.1 g| Sodium 808 mg | Carbs 6.8 g | Fiber 2.4g | Sugar 1.9g | Protein 61.2 g

Salmon with Green Beans

Prep: 12 Minutes | Cook Time: 18 Minutes | Makes: 1 Serving

Ingredients

- 1 salmon fillet, 2 inches thick
- 2 teaspoons of olive oil
- 2 teaspoons of smoked paprika
- Salt and black pepper, to taste
- 1 cup green beans
- Oil spray, for greasing

Directions

1. Grease the green beans with oil spray and set aside for further use,
2. Now rub the salmon fillet with olive oil, smoked paprika, salt, and black pepper.
3. Put the salmon fillets in the basket of air fryer along with green beans.
4. You can adjust the green beans on a rack as well.
5. Now set it to AIRFRY mode at 350 degrees F for 18 minutes.
6. Once done, take out the salmon and green beans and transfer them to the serving plates and enjoy.

Serving Suggestion: Serve it with ranch

Variation Tip: Use any other green vegetable of your choice

Nutritional Information Per Serving: Calories 367| Fat22 g| Sodium 87mg | Carbs 10.2g | Fiber 5.3g | Sugar 2g | Protein 37.2g

Fish and Chips

Prep: 15 Minutes | Cook Time: 22 Minutes | Makes: 2 Servings

Ingredients

- 1 pound of potatoes, cut lengthwise
- 1 cup seasoned flour
- 2 eggs, organic
- 1/3 cup buttermilk
- 2 cup seafood fry mix
- ½ cup bread crumbs
- 2 codfish fillet, 6 ounces each
- Oil spray, for greasing

Directions

1. Take a bowl and whisk eggs in it along   buttermilk.
2. In a separate bowl mix seafood fry mix and bread crumbs
3. Take a baking tray and spread flour on it
4. Dip the fillets first in egg wash, then in flour, and at the end coat it with breadcrumbs mixture.
5. Put the fish fillet in air fryer basket.
6. Grease the fish fillet with oil spray.
7. Put potato chips inside the basket and lightly grease it with oil spray.
8. Set the air fryer to AIR FRY mode at 400 degrees F for 22 minutes.
9. After 12 minutes take out the fish and continue with the cooking cycle.
10. Once done, serve and enjoy.

Serving Suggestion: Serve it with mayonnaise

Variation Tip: use water instead of buttermilk

Nutritional Information Per Serving: Calories 992| Fat 22.3g| Sodium1406 mg | Carbs 153.6g | Fiber 10g | Sugar10 g | Protein 40g

Spicy Fish Fillet with Onion Rings

Prep: 10 Minutes | Cook Time: 15 Minutes | Makes:1 Serving

Ingredients

- 300 grams of onion rings, frozen and packed
- 1 codfish fillet, 8 ounces
- Salt and black pepper, to taste
- 1 teaspoon of lemon juice
- oil spray, for greasing

Directions

1. Pat dry the fish fillets with a paper towel and season them with salt, black pepper, and lemon juice.
2. Grease the fillet with oil spray.
3. Put the fish in air fryer basket; adjust the onions rings besides.
4. Insert the basket into the unit.
5. Use AIRFRY mode at 350 degrees for 15 minutes.
6. Once done, serve hot.

Serving Suggestion: Serve with buffalo sauce

Variation Tip: None

Nutritional Information Per Serving: Calories 666| Fat23.5g| Sodium 911mg | Carbs 82g | Fiber 8.8g | Sugar 17.4g | Protein 30.4g

Salmon with Coconut

Prep: 10 Minutes | Cook Time: 12 Minutes | Makes: 2 Servings

Ingredients

- Oil spray, for greasing
- 2 salmon fillets, 6ounces each
- Salt and ground black pepper, to taste
- 1 tablespoon butter, for frying
- 1 tablespoon red curry paste
- 1 cup of coconut cream
- 2 tablespoons fresh cilantro, chopped
- 1 cup of cauliflower florets
- ½ cup Parmesan cheese, hard

Directions

1. Take a bowl and mix salt, black pepper, butter, red curry paste, coconut cream in a bowl and marinate the salmon in it.
2. Oil sprays the cauliflower florets and then seasons it with salt and freshly ground black pepper.
3. Put the florets in the air fryer basket and then place the salmon fillet aside.
4. Set it to AIR FRY mod at 12 minutes for4 00 degrees F
5. Once the time for cooking is over, serve the salmon with cauliflower floret with Parmesan cheese drizzle on top.

Serving Suggestion: Serve it with rice

Variation Tip: use mozzarella cheese instead of Parmesan cheese

Nutritional Information Per Serving: Calories 774 | Fat 59g| Sodium 1223mg | Carbs 12.2g | Fiber 3.9g | Sugar5.9 g | Protein53.5 g

Frozen Breaded Fish Fillet

Prep: 15 Minutes | Cook Time: 12 Minutes | Makes: 2 Servings

Ingredients

- 4 Frozen Breaded Fish Fillet
- Oil spray, for greasing
- 1 cup mayonnaise

Directions

1. Take the frozen fish fillets out of the bag and place them in the basket of the air fryer.
2. Lightly grease it with oil spray.
3. Set the unit to 380 degrees F fo12 minutes at AIR FRY mode.
4. Hit the start button to start cooking.
5. Once the cooking is done, serve the fish hot with mayonnaise.

Serving Suggestion: Serve it with salad and rice

Variation Tip: Use olive oil instead of butter

Nutritional Information per Serving:
Calories 921| Fat 61.5g| Sodium 1575mg | Carbs 69g | Fiber 2g | Sugar 9.5g | Protein 29.1g

Codfish with Herb Vinaigrette

Prep: 15 Minutes | Cook Time: 16 Minutes | Makes: 2 Servings

Ingredients

Vinaigrette Ingredients

- 1/2 cup parsley leaves
- 1 cup basil leaves
- ½ cup mint leaves
- 2 tablespoons thyme leaves
- 1/4 teaspoon red pepper flakes
- 2 cloves of garlic
- 4 tablespoons of red wine vinegar
- ¼ cup of olive oil
- Salt, to taste

Other Ingredients

- 1.5 pounds fish fillets, cod fish
- 2 tablespoons olive oil
- Salt and black pepper, to taste
- 1 teaspoon of paprika
- 1teasbpoon of Italian seasoning

Directions

1. Blend the entire vinaigrette ingredient in a high-speed blender and pulse into a smooth paste.
2. Set aside for drizzling overcooked fish.
3. Rub the fillets with salt, black pepper, paprika, Italian seasoning, and olive oil. Put it to the basket of the air fryer.
4. Set it to 16 minutes at 390 degrees F, at AIR FRY mode.
5. Once done, serve the fillets with the drizzle of blended vinaigrette

Serving Suggestion: Serve it with rice

Variation Tip: use sour cream instead of cream cheese

Nutritional Information Per Serving: Calories 1219| Fat 81.8g| Sodium 1906mg | Carbs64.4 g | Fiber5.5 g | Sugar 0.4g | Protein 52.1g

Beer Battered Fish Fillet

Prep: 18 Minutes | Cook Time: 14 Minutes | Makes: 2 Servings

Ingredients

- 1 cup all-purpose flour
- 4 tablespoons cornstarch
- 1 teaspoon baking soda
- 8 ounces beer
- 2 egg beaten
- ½ cup all-purpose flour
- 1 teaspoon smoked paprika
- 1 teaspoon salt
- 1/4 teaspoon freshly ground black pepper
- ¼ teaspoon of cayenne pepper
- 2 cod fillets, 1½-inches thick, cut into 4 pieces
- Oil spray, for greasing

Directions

1. Take a large bowl and combine flour, baking soda, corn starch, and salt
2. In a separate bowl beat eggs along with the beer.
3. In a shallow dish mix paprika, salt, pepper, and cayenne pepper.
4. Dry the codfish fillets with a paper towel.
5. Dip the fish into the eggs and coat it with seasoned flour.
6. Then dip it in the seasoning.
7. Grease the fillet with oil spray.
8. Put the fillets in air fryer basket.
9. Set it to AIR FRY mode at 400 degrees F for 14 minutes.
10. Press start and let the AIR fry do its magic.
11. Once cooking is done, serve the fish.
12. Enjoy it hot.

Serving Suggestion: Serve it with rice

Variation Tip: Use mild paprika instead of smoked paprika

Nutritional Information Per Serving: Calories 1691| Fat 6.1g| Sodium 3976mg | Carbs105.1 g | Fiber 3.4g | Sugar15.6 g | Protein 270g

Keto Baked Salmon with Pesto

Prep: 15 Minutes | Cook Time: 18 Minutes | Makes: 2 Servings

Ingredients

- 4 salmon fillets, 2 inches thick
- 2 ounces green pesto
- Salt and black pepper
- ½ tablespoon of canola oil, for greasing

Ingredients for Green Sauce

- 1-1/2 cup mayonnaise
- 2 tablespoons Greek yogurt
- Salt and black pepper, to taste

Directions

1. Rub the salmon with pesto, salt, oil, and black pepper.
2. In a small bowl, whisk together all the green sauce ingredients.
3. Put the fish fillets in the basket.
4. Set the AIR FRY mode for 18 minutes at 390 degrees F.
5. Once the cooking is done, serve it with green sauce drizzle.
6. Enjoy.

Serving Suggestion: Serve it with mashed cheesy potatoes

Variation Tip: Use butter instead of canal oil

Nutritional Information Per Serving: Calories 1165 | Fat80.7 g| Sodium 1087 mg | Carbs 33.1g | Fiber 0.5g | Sugar11.5 g | Protein 80.6g

Smoked Salmon

Prep: 20 Minutes | Cook Time: 12 Minutes | Makes: 4 Servings

Ingredients

- 2 pounds of salmon fillets, smoked
- 6 ounces cream cheese
- 4 tablespoons mayonnaise
- 2 teaspoons of chives, fresh
- 1 teaspoon of lemon zest
- Salt and freshly ground black pepper, to taste
- 2 tablespoons of butter

Directions

1. Cut the salmon into very small and uniform bite-size pieces.
2. Mix cream cheese, chives, mayonnaise, black pepper, and lemon zest, in a small mixing bowl.
3. Let it sit aside for further use.
4. Coat the salmon pieces with salt and butter.
5. Put it into the basket of the air fryer.
6. Set it on AIRFRY mode at 400 degrees F for 12 minutes.
7. Hit start, so the cooking starts.
8. Once the salmon is done, top it with a bowl creamy mixture and serve.
9. Enjoy hot.

Serving Suggestion: Serve it with rice

Variation Tip: use sour cream instead of cream cheese

Nutritional Information Per Serving: Calories 557| Fat 15.7 g| Sodium 371mg | Carbs 4.8 g | Fiber 0g | Sugar 1.1g | Protein 48 g

Two-Way Salmon

Prep: 10 Minutes | Cook Time: 18 Minutes | Makes: 2 Servings

Ingredients

- 2 salmon fillets, 8 ounces each
- 2 tablespoons of Cajun seasoning
- 2 tablespoons of jerk seasoning
- 1 lemon cut in half
- oil spray, for greasing

Directions

1. First, drizzle lemon juice over the salmon and wash it with tap water.
2. Rinse and pat dry the fillets with a paper towel.
3. Now rub o fillet with Cajun seasoning and grease it with oil spray.
4. Take the second fillet and rub it with jerk seasoning.
5. Grease the second fillet of salmon with oil spray.
6. Now put the salmon fillets in the air fryer basket.
7. Set the basket to 390 degrees F for 16-18 minutes at AIR FRY mode.
8. Hit the start button to start cooking.
9. Once the cooking is done, serve the fish fillets hot with mayonnaise.

Serving Suggestion: Serve it with ranch

Variation Tip: None

Nutritional Information Per Serving: Calories 238| Fat 11.8g| Sodium 488mg | Carbs 9g | Fiber 0g | Sugar8 g | Protein 35g

Lemon Pepper Salmon with Asparagus

Prep: 20 Minutes | Cook Time: 20 Minutes | Makes: 2 Servings

Ingredients

- 1 cup of green asparagus
- 2 tablespoons of butter
- 2 fillets of salmon, 8 ounces each
- Salt and black pepper, to taste
- 1 teaspoon of lemon juice
- ½ teaspoon of lemon zest
- oil spray, for greasing

Directions

1. Rinse and trim the asparagus.
2. Rinse and pat dry the salmon fillets.
3. Take a bowl and mix lemon juice, lemon zest, salt, and black pepper.
4. Brush the fish fillet with the rub and place it in the basket along with asparagus.
5. Set it to AIRFRY mode for 20 minutes at 390 degrees F.
6. Once 5 minutes pass take out the basket and remove asparagus.
7. Continue with the cooking cycle..
8. Once done, serve and enjoy.

Serving Suggestion: Serve it with baked potato

Variation Tip: Use olive oil instead of butter.

Nutritional Information Per Serving: Calories 482| Fat 28g| Sodium209 mg | Carbs 2.8g | Fiber1.5 g | Sugar1.4 g | Protein 56.3g

Chapter 7-Vegetables Recipes

Stuffed Tomatoes

Prep: 12 Minutes | Cook Time: 8 Minutes | Makes: 2 Servings

Ingredients

- 2 cups brown rice, cooked
- 1 cup of tofu, grilled and chopped
- 4 large red tomatoes
- 4 tablespoons basil, chopped
- 1/4 tablespoon olive oil
- Salt and black pepper, to taste
- 2 tablespoons of lemon juice
- 1 teaspoon of red chili powder
- ½ cup Parmesan cheese

Directions

1. Take a large bowl and mix rice, tofu, basil, olive oil, salt, black pepper, lemon juice, and chili powder.
2. Take four large tomatoes and center core them.
3. Fill the cavity with the rice mixture.
4. Top it off with the cheese sprinkle.
5. Put the tomatoes into the air fryer basket.
6. Set it to AIRFRY mode, for 8 minutes at 400 degrees F.
7. Once done, serve and enjoy.

Serving Suggestion: Serve it with Greek yogurt

Variation Tip: Use canola oil instead of olive oil.

Nutritional Information Per Serving: Calories 1034| Fat 24.2g| Sodium 527mg | Carbs165 g | Fiber12.1 g | Sugar 1.2g | Protein 43.9g

Zucchini with Stuffing

Prep: 12 Minutes | Cook Time: 20 Minutes | Makes: 3 Servings

Ingredients

- 1 cup quinoa, rinsed
- 1 cup black olives
- 6 medium zucchinis, about 2 pounds
- 2 cups cannellini beans, drained
- 1 white onion, chopped
- ¼ cup almonds, chopped
- 4 cloves of garlic, chopped
- 4 tablespoons olive oil
- 1 cup of water
- 2 cups Parmesan cheese, for topping

Directions

1. First wash the zucchini and cut it lengthwise.
2. Take a skillet and heat oil in it
3. Sauté the onion in olive oil for a few minutes.
4. Then add the quinoa and water and let it cook for 8 minutes with the lid on the top.
5. Transfer the quinoa to a bowl and add all remaining ingredients excluding zucchini and Parmesan cheese.
6. Scoop out the seeds of zucchinis.
7. Fill the cavity of zucchinis with bowl mixture.
8. Top it with a handful of Parmesan cheese.
9. Arrange 4 zucchinis in the air fryer basket.
10. Select the AIR FRY for 20 minutes and adjust the temperature to 390 degrees F.
11. Once done, serve and enjoy.

Serving Suggestion: Serve it with pasta

Variation Tip: None

Nutritional Information Per Serving: Calories 1171| Fat 48.6g| Sodium 1747mg | Carbs 132.4g | Fiber 42.1g | Sugar 11.5g | Protein 65.7g

Green Beans with Baked Potatoes

Prep: 15 Minutes | Cook Time: 45 Minutes | Makes: 2 Servings

Ingredients

- 2 cups of green beans
- 2 large potatoes, cubed
- 3 tablespoons of olive oil
- 1 teaspoon of seasoned salt
- ½ teaspoon chili powder
- 1/6 teaspoon garlic powder
- 1/4 teaspoon onion powder

Directions

1. Take a large bowl and pour olive oil into it.
2. Now add all the seasoning in the olive oil and whisk it well.
3. Toss the green bean in it, and then transfer it to the basket of the air fryer.
4. Now season the potatoes with the seasoning and add them to the basket as well.
5. Now set the unit to AIRFRY mode at 350 degrees F for 45 minutes.
6. After 18 minutes take out the asparagus and continue with cooking.
7. Once the cooking cycle is complete, take out and serve it by transferring it to the serving plates.

Serving Suggestion: serve with rice

Variation Tip: use canola oil instead of olive oil

Nutritional Information Per Serving: Calories473 | Fat21.6g | Sodium796 mg | Carbs 66.6g | Fiber12.9 g | Sugar6 g | Protein8.4 g

Cheesy Potatoes with Asparagus

Prep: 15 Minutes | Cook Time: 35 Minutes | Makes: 2 Servings

Ingredients

- 1-1/2 pounds of russet potato, wedges or cut in half
- 2 teaspoons mixed herbs
- 2 teaspoons chili flakes
- 2 cups asparagus
- 1 cup chopped onion
- 1 tablespoon Dijon mustard
- 1/4 cup fresh cream
- 1 teaspoon olive oil
- 2 tablespoons of butter
- 1/2 teaspoon salt and black pepper
- Water as required
- 1/2 cup Parmesan cheese

Directions

1. Take a bowl and add asparagus and sweet potato wedges to it.
2. Season it with salt, black pepper, and olive oil.
3. Now add the potato wedges to the air fryer basket along with the asparagus.
4. Set it to AIRFRY mode at 390 degrees F for 30 minutes.
5. Meanwhile, take a skillet and add butter and sauté onion in it for a few minutes.
6. Then add salt and Dijon mustard and chili flakes, Parmesan cheese, and fresh cream.
7. Once cooking time passes 12 minutes, take out asparagus and continue cooking cycle.
8. Once it's done, take out the potato wedges.
9. Drizzle the skillet ingredients over the potatoes and serve with asparagus.

Serving Suggestion: Serve with rice

Variation Tip: Use olive oil instead of butter

Nutritional Information Per Serving: Calories 251| Fat11g | Sodium 279mg | Carbs 31.1g | Fiber 5g | Sugar 4.1g | Protein9 g

Kale and Spinach Chips

Prep: 12 Minutes | Cook Time: 8 Minutes | Makes: 2 Servings

Ingredients

- 2 cups spinach, torn in pieces and stem removed
- 2 cups kale, torn in pieces, stems removed
- 1 tablespoon of olive oil
- Sea salt, to taste
- 1/3 cup Parmesan cheese

Directions

1. Take a bowl and add spinach to it.
2. Take another bowl and add kale to it.
3. Now, season both of them with olive oil, and sea salt.
4. Add kale and spinach to the basket of air fryer.
5. Select the air fry mode at 350 degrees F for 8 minutes.
6. Once done, take out the crispy chips and sprinkle Parmesan cheese on top.
7. Serve and Enjoy.

Serving Suggestion: Serve it with baked potato

Variation Tip: use canola oil instead of olive oil

Nutritional Information Per Serving: Calories 166| Fat 11.1g| Sodium 355mg | Carbs 8.1g | Fiber1.7 g | Sugar 0.1g | Protein 8.2g

Mixed Air Fry Veggies

Prep: 15 Minutes | Cook Time: 25 Minutes | Makes: 4 Servings

Ingredients

- 2 cups of carrots, cubed
- 2 cups of potatoes, cubed
- 2 cups of shallots, cubed
- 2 cups zucchini, diced
- 2 cups yellow squash, cubed
- Salt and black pepper, to taste
- 1 tablespoon of Italian seasoning
- 2 tablespoons of ranch seasoning
- 4 tablespoons of olive oil

Directions

1. Take a large bowl and add all the veggies to it.
2. Season the veggies with salt, pepper, Italian seasoning, ranch seasoning, and olive oil
3. Toss all the ingredients well.
4. Now put it to the basket of the air fryer.
5. Set the unit to AIRFRY mode at 360 degrees F for 25 minutes.
6. Once it is cooked and done, serve, and enjoy.

Serving Suggestion: Serve it with rice

Variation Tip: None

Nutritional Information Per Serving: Calories 275| Fat 15.3g| Sodium129 mg | Carbs 33g | Fiber3.8 g | Sugar5 g | Protein 4.4g

Garlic Herbed Baked Potatoes

Prep: 25 Minutes | Cook Time: 45 Minutes | Makes: 4 Servings

Ingredients

- 4 large baking potatoes
- Salt and black pepper, to taste
- 2 teaspoons of avocado oil

Cheese ingredients

- 2 cups sour cream
- 1 teaspoon of garlic clove, minced
- 1 teaspoon fresh dill
- 2 teaspoons chopped chives
- Salt and black pepper, to taste
- 2 teaspoons Worcestershire sauce

Directions

1. Pierce the skin of potatoes with a fork.
2. Season the potatoes with olive oil, salt, and black pepper.
3. Put the potatoes into the basket of the ninja air fryer.
4. Now set it to AIR FRY mode at 350 degrees F, for 45 minutes.
5. Meanwhile, take a bowl and mix all the ingredient under cheese ingredients
6. Once the cooking cycle complete, take out and make a slit in-between the potatoes.
7. Add cheese mixture in the cavity and serve it hot.

Serving Suggestion: serve with gravy

Variation Tip: None

Nutritional Information Per Serving: Calories 382| Fat24.6 g| Sodium 107mg | Carbs 36.2g | Fiber 2.5g | Sugar2 g | Protein 7.3g

Garlic Potato Wedges in Air Fryer

Prep: 10 Minutes | Cook Time: 20 Minutes | Makes: 2 Servings

Ingredients

- 4 medium potatoes, peeled and cut into wedges
- 4 tablespoons of butter
- 1 teaspoon of chopped cilantro
- 1 cup plain flour
- 1 teaspoon of garlic, minced
- Salt and black pepper, to taste

Directions

1. Soak the potatoes wedges in cold water for about 30 minutes.
2. Then drain and pat dry with a paper towel.
3. Boil water in a large pot and boil the wedges just for 3 minutes.
4. Then take it out on a paper towel.
5. Now in bowl mix garlic, melted butter, salt, pepper, cilantro and whisk it well.
6. Add the flour to a separate bowl and add salt and black pepper.
7. Then add water to the flour so it gets runny in texture.
8. Now, coat the potatoes with flour mixture and add it to a foil tin.
9. Put foil tin in the air fryer basket.
10. Now, set time using AIRFRY mode at 390 degrees F for 20 minutes.
11. Once done, serve and enjoy.

Serving Suggestion: Serve with ketchup

Variation Tip: use olive oil instead of butter

Nutritional Information Per Serving: Calories 727| Fat 24.1g| Sodium 191mg | Carbs 115.1g | Fiber 12g | Sugar 5.1g | Protein14 g

Fresh Mix Veggies in Air Fryer

Prep: 15minutes | Cook Time: 12 Minutes | Makes: 4 Servings

Ingredients

- 1 cup cauliflower florets
- 1 cup of carrots, peeled chopped
- 1 cup broccoli florets
- 2 tablespoons of avocado oil
- Salt, to taste
- ½ teaspoon of chili powder
- ½ teaspoon of garlic powder
- ½ teaspoon of herbs de Provence
- 1 cup parmesan cheese

Directions

1. Take a bowl, and add all the veggies to it.
2. Toss and then season the veggies with salt, chili powder, garlic powder, and herbs de Provence.
3. Toss it all well and then drizzle avocado oil.
4. Make sure the ingredients are coated well.
5. Now transfer the veggies to the basket of the air fryer.
6. Turn on the start button and set it to AIR FRY mode at 390 degrees for 10-12 minutes.
7. After 8 minutes of cooking, select the pause button and then take out the basket and sprinkle Parmesan cheese on top of the veggies.
8. Then let the cooking cycle complete for the next 3-4 minutes.
9. Once done, serve.

Serving Suggestion: Serve it with rice

Variation Tip: Use canola oil or Butter instead of avocado oil

Nutritional Information Per Serving: Calories161 | Fat 9.3g| Sodium434 mg | Carbs 7.7g | Fiber 2.4g | Sugar 2.5g | Protein 13.9

Brussels sprouts

Prep: 15 Minutes | Cook Time: 20 Minutes | Makes: 2 Servings

Ingredients

- 2 pounds Brussels sprouts
- 2 tablespoons avocado oil
- Salt and pepper, to taste
- 1 cup pine nuts, roasted

Directions

1. Trim the bottom of Brussels sprouts.
2. Take a bowl and combine the avocado oil, salt, and black pepper.
3. Toss the Brussels sprouts well.
4. Transfer it to the air fryer basket.
5. Use AIR fry mode for 20 minutes at 390 degrees F.
6. Once the Brussels sprouts get crisp and tender, take out and serve.

Serving Suggestion: Serve with Rice

Variation Tip: Use olive oil instead of avocado oil

Nutritional Information Per Serving: Calories 672| Fat 50g| Sodium 115mg | Carbs 51g | Fiber 20.2g | Sugar 12.3g | Protein 25g

Chapter 8-Desserts Recipes

Cake in The Air Fryer

Prep: 12 Minutes | Cook Time: 30 Minutes | Makes: 2 Servings

Ingredients

- 90 grams all-purpose flour
- Pinch of salt
- 1/2 teaspoon of baking powder
- ½ cup of tutti fruitti mix
- 2 eggs
- 1 teaspoon of vanilla extract
- 10 tablespoons of white sugar

Directions

1. Take a bowl and add all-purpose flour, salt, and baking powder.
2. Stir it in a large bowl.
3. Whisk two eggs in a separate bowl and add vanilla extract, sugar and blend it with a hand beater.
4. Now combine wet ingredients with the dry ones.
5. Mix it well and pour it into round pan that fits inside basket.
6. Place the pan inside the basket.
7. Now set it to BAKE function at 310 for 30 minutes.
8. Once it's done, serve and enjoy.

Serving Suggestion: Serve it with whipped cream

Variation Tip: Use brown sugar instead of white sugar

Nutritional Information Per Serving: Calories 711| Fat4.8g| Sodium 143mg | Carbs 161g | Fiber 1.3g | Sugar 105g | Protein 10.2g

Bread Pudding

Prep: 12 Minutes | Cook Time: 8-12 Minutes | Makes: 2 Servings

Ingredients

- Nonstick spray, for greasing ramekins
- 2 slices of white bread, crumbled
- 4 tablespoons of white sugar
- 5 large eggs
- ½ cup cream
- Salt, pinch
- 1/3 teaspoon of cinnamon powder

Directions

1. Take a bowl and whisk eggs in it.
2. Add sugar and salt to the egg and whisk it all well.
3. Then add cream and use a hand beater to incorporate the entire ingredients.
4. Now add cinnamon, and add crumbs of bread.
5. Mix it well and add into a round shaped baking pan.
6. Put it inside the ninja air fryer.
7. Set it on AIRFRY mode at 350 degrees F for 8-12 minutes.
8. Once it's cooked, serve.

Serving Suggestion: Serve it with Coffee

Variation Tip: Use brown sugar instead of white sugar

Nutritional Information Per Serving: Calories 331| Fat16.1g| Sodium 331mg | Carbs 31g | Fiber0.2g | Sugar 26.2g | Protein 16.2g

Air Fryer Sweet Twists

Prep: 15 Minutes | Cook Time: 10 Minutes | Makes: 2 Servings

Ingredients

- 1 box store-bought puff pastry
- ½ teaspoon cinnamon
- ½ teaspoon sugar
- ½ teaspoon black sesame seeds
- Salt, pinch
- 2 tablespoons Parmesan cheese, freshly grated

Directions

1. Place the dough on a work surface.
2. Take a small bowl and mix cheese, sugar, salt, sesame seeds, and cinnamon.
3. Press this mixture on both sides of the dough.
4. Now, cut the pastry into 1" x 3" strips.
5. Twist each of the strips 2 times and then lay it onto the flat.
6. Transfer it to the air fryer basket.
7. Select the air fry mode at 400 degrees F for 10 minutes.
8. Once cooked, serve.

Serving Suggestion: Serve it with champagne!

Variation Tip: None

Nutritional Information Per Serving: Calories 140| Fat9.4g| Sodium 142mg | Carbs 12.3g | Fiber0.8 g | Sugar 1.2g | Protein 2g

Pumpkin Muffins

Prep: 20 Minutes | Cook Time: 19 Minutes | Makes: 4 Servings

Ingredients

- 1 and ½ cups of all-purpose flour
- ½ teaspoon baking soda
- ½ teaspoon of baking powder
- 1 and 1/4 teaspoons cinnamon, groaned
- 1/4 teaspoon ground nutmeg, grated
- 2 large eggs
- Salt, pinch
- 3/4 cup granulated sugar
- 1/2 cup dark brown sugar
- 1 and 1/2 cups of pumpkin puree
- 1/4 cup coconut milk

Directions

1. Take 4 ramekins that are the size of a cup and layer them with muffin papers.
2. Crack an egg in a bowl and add brown sugar, baking soda, baking powder, cinnamon, nutmeg, and sugar.
3. Whisk it all very well with an electric hand beater.
4. Now, in a second bowl, mix the flour, and salt.
5. Now, mix the dry ingredients slowly with the wet ingredients.
6. Now, at the end fold in the pumpkin puree and milk, mix it well
7. Divide this batter into 4 ramekins.
8. Now, put the ramekins inside the basket.
9. Add basket to the unit.
10. Set the time to 18 minutes at 360 degrees Fat AIRFRY mode.
11. Check if not done, and let it AIR FRY for one more minute.
12. Once it is done, serve.

Serving Suggestion: Serve it with a glass of milk

Variation Tip: Use almond milk instead of coconut milk

Nutritional Information Per Serving: Calories 291| Fat6.4 g| Sodium 241mg | Carbs 57.1g | Fiber 4.4g | Sugar42 g | Protein 5.9g

Lemony Sweet Twists

Prep: 15 Minutes | Cook Time: 9 Minutes | Makes: 2 Servings

Ingredients

- 1 box store-bought puff pastry
- ½ teaspoon lemon zest
- 1 tablespoon of lemon juice
- 2 teaspoons brown sugar
- Salt, pinch
- 2 tablespoons Parmesan cheese, freshly grated

Directions

1. Put the puff pastry dough on a clean work area.
2. In a bowl, combine Parmesan cheese, brown sugar, salt, lemon zest, and lemon juice.
3. Press this mixture on both sides of the dough.
4. Now, cut the pastry into 1" x 4" strips.
5. Twist each of the strips.
6. Transfer it to the air fryer basket.
7. Select the air fry mode at 400 degrees F for 9-10 minutes..
8. Once cooked, serve and enjoy.

Serving Suggestion: Serve it with champagne!

Variation Tip: None

Nutritional Information Per Serving: Calories 156| Fat10g| Sodium 215mg | Carbs 14g | Fiber 0.4g | Sugar3.3 g | Protein 2.8g

Fudge Brownies

Prep: 20 Minutes | Cook Time: 35 Minutes | Makes: 4 Servings

Ingredients

- 1/2 cup all-purpose flour
- 1/4 cup unsweetened cocoa powder
- 3/4 teaspoon kosher salt
- 2 large eggs, whisked
- 1 tablespoon almond milk
- 1/2 cup brown sugar
- 1/2 cup packed white sugar
- 1/2 tablespoon vanilla extract
- 8 ounces of semisweet chocolate chips, melted
- 2/4 cup unsalted butter, melted

Directions

1. Take a medium bowl, and use a hand beater to whisk together eggs, milk, both the sugars and vanilla.
2. In a separate microwave-safe bowl, mix melted butter and chocolate and microwave it for 30 seconds to melt the chocolate.
3. Add all the listed dry ingredients to the chocolate mixture.
4. Now incorporate the egg bowl ingredient into the batter.
5. Spray a reasonable size round baking pan that fits in basket of air fryer.
6. Grease the pan with cooking spray.
7. Now pour the batter into the pan, put the crisper plate in basket.
8. Add the pan and insert the basket into the unit.
9. Select the AIR FRY mode and adjust the setting the temperature to 300 degrees F, for 30 minutes.
10. Check it after 35 minutes and if not done, cook for 10 more minutes
11. Once it's done, take it out and let it get cool before serving.
12. Enjoy.

Serving Suggestion: Serve it with a dollar of the vanilla ice cream

Variation Tip: Use dairy milk instead of almond milk

Nutritional Information Per Serving: Calories 760| Fat43.3 g| Sodium644 mg | Carbs 93.2g | Fiber5.3 g | Sugar 70.2g | Protein 6.2g

Chocolate Chip Muffins

Prep: 12 Minutes | Cook Time: 15 Minutes | Makes: 2 Servings

Ingredients

- Salt, pinch
- 2 eggs
- 1/3 cup brown sugar
- 1/3 cup butter
- 4 tablespoons of milk
- ¼ teaspoon of vanilla extract
- ½ teaspoon of baking powder
- 1 cup all-purpose flour
- 1 pouch chocolate chips, 35 grams

Directions

1. Take 4 oven-safe ramekins that are the size of a cup and layer them with muffin papers.
2. In a bowl, whisk the egg, brown sugar, butter, milk, and vanilla extract.
3. Whisk it all very well with an electric hand beater.
4. Now, in a second bowl, mix the flour, baking powder, and salt.
5. Now, mix the dry ingredients slowly into the wet ingredients.
6. Now, at the end fold in the chocolate chips and mix them well
7. Divide this batter into 4 ramekins.
8. Now, put the ramekins in the basket.
9. Set the time to 15 minutes at 350 degrees F, at AIRFRY mode.
10. Check if not done, and let it AIR FRY for one more minute.
11. Once it is done, serve.

Serving Suggestion: Serve it with chocolate syrup drizzle

Variation Tip: None

Nutritional Information Per Serving: Calories 757| Fat40.3g| Sodium 426mg | Carbs 85.4g | Fiber 2.2g | Sugar 30.4g | Protein 14.4g

Chocolate Chip Cake

Prep: 12 Minutes | Cook Time: 15 Minutes | Makes: 4servings

Ingredients

- Salt, pinch
- 2 eggs, whisked
- ½ cup brown sugar
- ½ cup butter, melted
- 10 tablespoons of almond milk
- ¼ teaspoon of vanilla extract
- ½ teaspoon of baking powder
- 1 cup all-purpose flour
- 1 cup of chocolate chips
- ½ cup of cocoa powder

Directions

1. Take a large baking pan that fits inside the basket of the air fryer.
2. Layer it with baking paper, cut it to the size of a baking pan.
3. In a bowl, whisk the egg, brown sugar, butter, almond milk, and vanilla extract.
4. Whisk it all very well with an electric hand beater.
5. In a second bowl, mix the flour, cocoa powder, baking powder, and salt.
6. Now, mix the dry ingredients slowly with the wet ingredients.
7. Now, at the end fold in the chocolate chips.
8. Incorporate all the ingredients well.
9. Pour this batter into the round baking pan.
10. put it inside the basket.
11. Set the time to 15 minutes at 350 degrees F at AIR FRY mode.
12. Check if not done, and let it AIR FRY for one more minute.
13. Once it is done, serve.

Serving Suggestion: Serve it with chocolate syrup drizzle

Variation Tip: Use baking soda instead of baking powder

Nutritional Information Per Serving: Calories 736| Fat45.5g| Sodium 356mg | Carbs 78.2g | Fiber 6.1g | Sugar 32.7g | Protein11.5 g

Mini Blueberry Pies

Prep: 12 Minutes | Cook Time: 10 Minutes | Makes: 2 Servings

Ingredients

- 1 box Store-Bought Pie Dough, Trader Joe's
- ¼ cup blueberry jam
- 1 teaspoon of lemon zest
- 1 egg white, for brushing

Directions

1. Take the store brought pie dough and cut it into 3-inch circles.
2. Brush the dough with egg white all around the parameters.
3. Now add blueberry jam and zest in the middle and top it with another circular.
4. Press the edges with the fork to seal it.
5. Make a slit in the middle of the dough and transfer it to the basket.
6. Set it to AIR FRY mode at 360 degrees for 10 minutes.
7. Once cooked, serve.

Serving Suggestion: Serve it with vanilla ice-cream

Variation Tip: use orange zest instead of lemon zest

Nutritional Information Per Serving: Calories 234| Fat8.6g| Sodium187 mg | Carbs 38.2 g | Fiber 0.1g | Sugar13.7 g | Protein 2g

Mini Strawberry and Cream Pies

Prep: 12 Minutes | Cook Time: 10 Minutes | Makes: 2 Servings

Ingredients

- 1 box Store-Bought Pie Dough, Trader Joe's
- 1 cup strawberries, cubed
- 3 tablespoons of cream, heavy
- 2 tablespoons of almonds
- 1 egg white, for brushing

Directions

1. Take the store brought pie dough and flatten it on a surface.
2. Use a round cutter to cut it into 3-inch circles.
3. Brush the dough with egg white all around the parameters.
4. Now add almonds, strawberries, and cream in a very little amount in the center of the dough, and top it with another circular.
5. Press the edges with the fork to seal it.
6. Make a slit in the middle of the dough and put it into the basket.
7. Set it to AIR FRY mode 360 degrees for 10 minutes.
8. Once done, serve.

Serving Suggestion: Serve it with vanilla ice-cream

Variation Tip: use orange zest instead of lemon zest

Nutritional Information Per Serving: Calories 203| Fat12.7g| Sodium 193mg | Carbs20 g | Fiber 2.2g | Sugar 5.8g | Protein 3.7g

Chapter 9-3 Weeks Diet Plan

Days	Breakfast	Lunch	Dinner
Day1	BREAKFAST SAUSAGE OMELET &SWEET BITES	CHICKEN THIGHS WITH BRUSSELS SPROUTS & CHEDDAR QUICHE	FISH AND CHIPS & KALE AND SPINACH CHIPS
Day 2	YELLOW POTATOES WITH EGGS & STRAWBERRIES AND WALNUTS MUFFINS	CHICKEN & BROCCOLI & BRUSSELS SPROUTS	SPICE-RUBBED CHICKEN PIECES & MIXED AIR FRY VEGGIES
Day 3	EGG WITH BABY SPINACH&GRILL CHEESE SANDWICH	SPICY CHICKEN &KALE AND SPINACH CHIPS	BEER BATTERED FISH FILLET & CHEESY POTATOES WITH ASPARAGUS
Day 4	SWEET POTATOES HASH& DIJON CHEESE SANDWICH	SPICY FISH FILLET WITH ONION RINGS &BRUSSELS SPROUTS	FROZEN BREADED FISH FILLET & MIXED AIR FRY VEGGIES
Day 5	BANANA AND RAISINS MUFFINS& GRILL CHEESE SANDWICH	CHICKEN & BROCCOLI & SALMON WITH GREEN BEANS	BEEF & BROCCOLI & STUFFED TOMATOES
Day 6	EGG WITH BABY	TWO-WAY SALMON &	YUMMY CHICKEN BREASTS &STUFFED TOMATOES

	SPINACH&GRILL CHEESE SANDWICH	SPICED CHICKEN AND VEGETABLES	
Day 7	SWEET POTATOES HASH &DIJON CHEESE SANDWICH	CHICKEN BREAST STRIPS &Keto Baked Salmon With Pesto	STEAK AND MASHED CREAMY POTATOES & ZUCCHINI WITH STUFFING
Day 8	YELLOW POTATOES WITH EGGS &BLUEBERRIES MUFFINS	WINGS WITH CORN ON COB & BRUSSELS SPROUTS	CHICKEN LEG PIECE &STUFFED TOMATOES
Day 9	EGG AND AVOCADO IN THE NINJA FOODI &DIJON CHEESE SANDWICH	SPICE-RUBBED CHICKEN PIECES & BRUSSELS SPROUTS	CHINESE BBQ PORK & CHEESY POTATOES WITH ASPARAGUS
Day 10	BACON AND EGG OMELET &BLUEBERRIES MUFFINS	SPICY FISH FILLET WITH ONION RINGS	SHORT RIBS & ROOT VEGETABLES
Day 11	EGG WITH BABY SPINACH &BLUEBERRIES MUFFINS	FISH AND CHIPS & BRUSSELS SPROUTS	PORK CHOPS & FRESH MIX VEGGIES IN AIR FRYER
Day 12	YELLOW POTATOES WITH EGGS&GRILL	CHICKEN & BROCCOLI & STUFFED TOMATOES	GLAZED STEAK RECIPE &ZUCCHINI WITH STUFFING

	CHEESE SANDWICH		
Day 13	SWEET POTATOES HASH &GRILL CHEESE SANDWICH	WINGS WITH CORN ON COB & ZUCCHINI WITH STUFFING	STEAK IN AIR FRY & GARLIC HERBED BAKED POTATOES
Day 14	EGG AND AVOCADO IN THE NINJA FOODI & BLUEBERRIES MUFFINS	GLAZED THIGHS WITH FRENCH FRIES &BRUSSELS SPROUTS	YOGURT LAMB CHOPS & CHEESY POTATOES WITH ASPARAGUS
Day 15	BANANA AND RAISINS MUFFINS &DIJON CHEESE SANDWICH	GLAZED THIGHS WITH FRENCH FRIES	HAM BURGER PATTIES & GARLIC HERBED BAKED POTATOES
Day 16	BACON AND EGG OMELET & DIJON CHEESE SANDWICH	CHEDDAR QUICHE & GARLIC HERBED BAKED POTATOES	FROZEN BREADED FISH FILLET & Garlic Potato Wedges In Air Fryer
Day 17	BACON AND EGGS FOR BREAKFAST &BLUEBERRIES MUFFINS	CHICKEN WINGS & Garlic Potato Wedges In Air Fryer	SPICY LAMB CHOPS & STUFFED TOMATOES
Day 18	SAUSAGE WITH EGGS	BELL PEPPERS WITH SAUSAGES	BEEF RIBS &

	&GRILL CHEESE SANDWICH	&GREEN BEANS WITH BAKED POTATOES	GARLIC HERBED BAKED POTATOES
Day 19	BREAKFAST SAUSAGE OMELET &BLUEBERRIES MUFFINS	BEEF RIBS & GREEN BEANS WITH BAKED POTATOES	BELL PEPPERS WITH SAUSAGES & STUFFED TOMATOES
Day 20	BACON AND EGG OMELET & BLUEBERRIES MUFFINS	GLAZED THIGHS WITH FRENCH FRIES & STUFFED TOMATOES	SPICY LAMB CHOPS & FRESH MIX VEGGIES IN AIR FRYER
Day 21	BREAKFAST CASSEROLE &GRILL CHEESE SANDWICH	CHEDDAR QUICHE & GARLIC HERBED BAKED POTATOES	HAM BURGER PATTIES &STUFFED TOMATOES

Conclusion

Now making a crispy and low-fat meal is no more of a hustle, as this cookbook introduces some scrumptious recipe collection that you can prepare anytime by using a Ninja Foodi Air Fryer.

Once you buy this appliance, you will need no other traditional appliance for baking, roasting, rehydrating, and reheating. We hope that you are impressed by its functionality, operation, and one-touch technology.

Moreover, we have written the cookbook comprehensively by ditching the fluffy.
All the necessary information regarding the use of air fryer is in this cookbook.
Now, as a beginner, you can prepare some delicious homemade recipes.

We highly recommend buying one for you.

Printed in Great Britain
by Amazon